SKYSCRAPERS
STRUCTURE AND DESIGN

MATTHEW WELLS

SKYSCRAPERS
STRUCTURE AND DESIGN

YALE UNIVERSITY PRESS

Published in North America by
Yale University Press
P.O. Box 209040
New Haven, CT 06520-9040
U.S.A.

First published in Great Britain in 2005 by
Laurence King Publishing Ltd, London

Library of Congress Control Number:
2004113044

ISBN 0-300-10679-3

Managing editor Mark Fletcher
Design Neil Pereira
Copy editor Ian McDonald
Picture research Claire Gouldstone

Printed in China

CONTENTS

CASE STUDIES

Wing Tower
Glasgow, UK, 1999
Architect: Richard Horden
Engineer: Buro Happold

Swiss Re Headquarters
London, UK, 2002
Architect: Foster and Partners
Engineer: Arup

London Bridge Tower
London, UK, in progress
Architect: Renzo Piano Building
Workshop/Broadway Malyan
Engineer: Arup

Grand Union Building
London, UK, 2003
Architect: Richard Rogers Partnership
Engineer: Pell Frischmann

Heron Tower
London, UK, 2006
Architect: Kohn Pedersen Fox
Engineer: Arup

The Spire of Dublin
Dublin, Ireland, 2003
Architect: Ian Ritchie Architects
Engineer: Arup

Tour sans Fin
Paris, France, unbuilt
Architect: Atelier Jean Nouvel
Engineer: Arup

Torre Agbar
Barcelona, Spain, 2004
Architect: Atelier Jean Nouvel
Engineer: Brufau/Obiol

**Hotel Habitat, Hotel Hesperia
and Office Towers**
Barcelona, Spain, 2005
Architect: Dominique Perrault
Engineer: Brufau/Pamias Industrial Engineering

Commerzbank
Frankfurt, Germany, 1997
Architect: Foster and Partners
Engineer: Arup

Debis House, Potsdamer Platz
Berlin, Germany, 1999
Architect: Renzo Piano Building
Workshop/Christoph Kohlbecker
Engineer: Boll and Partner

Deutsche Post
Bonn, Germany, 1999
Architects: Murphy/Jahn
Engineers: Werner Sobek

Colorium
Düsseldorf, Germany, 2001
Architect: Alsop Architects
Engineer: Arup GmbH

Uptown München
Munich, Germany, 2003
Architect: Ingenhoven Overdiek Architekten
Engineer: Burggraf, Weichinger and Partner

Bergisel Ski Jump
Innsbruck, Austria, 2002
Architect: Zaha Hadid Architects
Engineer: Jane Wernick/Christian Aste

Twin Towers
Vienna, Austria, 2001
Architect: Massimiliano Fuksas
Engineer: Büro Thumberger + Kressmeier

Montevideo
Rotterdam, The Netherlands, 2005
Architect: Mecanoo Architecten
Engineer: ABT

Turning Torso
Malmö, Sweden, 2005
Architect: Santiago Calatrava
Engineer: Santiago Calatrava SA

Stratosphere Tower
Las Vegas, USA, 1996
Architect: Gary Wilson
Engineer: Brent Wright

Condé Nast Tower
New York, USA, 2002
Architect: Fox and Fowle Architects
Engineer: Ysrael Seinuk

New York Times Building
New York, USA, 2004
Architect: Renzo Piano Building Workshop/Fox
and Fowle Architects
Engineer: Thornton-Tomasetti Engineers

AOL Time Warner Center
New York, USA, 2003
Architect: Skidmore, Owings and Merrill LLP
Engineer: Cantor Seinuk

Highcliff
Hong Kong, 2002
Architect: Dennis Lau and Ng
Chun Man Architects
Engineer: Magnusson Klemencic
Associates/Maunsell Group

International Finance Centre II
Hong Kong, 2003
Architect: Cesar Pelli and Associates/
Rocco Design
Engineer: Arup, Hong Kong

Di Wang Commercial Centre
Shenzhen, China, 1996
Architect: K.Y. Cheung Design Associates
Engineer: Leslie E. Robertson/Maunsell

Taipei Financial Centre
Taipei, Taiwan, 2004
Architect: C.Y. Lee Partners
Engineer: Evergreen Consulting Engineering

Petronas Towers
Kuala Lumpur, Malaysia, 1997
Architect: Cesar Pelli and Associates
Engineer: Thornton-Tomasetti Engineers/
Ranhill Bersekutu

Menara UMNO
Penang Island, Malaysia, 1998
Architect: T. R. Hamzah and Yeang
Engineer: Tahir Wong

Burj Al Arab Hotel
Dubai, United Arab Emirates, 1996
Architect: W.S. Atkins and Partners
Engineer: W.S. Atkins and Partners

The Great Lighthouse, or Pharos, of Alexandria – the tallest structure in the ancient world – was built by Alexander the Great just outside the entrance to his new city's harbour. The structure needed to be seen from about 50 kilometres (35 miles) away, in good time for approaching vessels to make a realignment. The Pharos was made 200 metres (650 feet) tall, slightly higher than the Great Pyramid of Cheops, sited 320 kilometres (200 miles) to the south. Despite the structural sophistication of the pyramids, with their multiple cores of masonry worked out within a mere two generations, the Theban-granite-clad Pharos appears the more astounding technology today.

A fire was kept burning on the tower day and night, the smoke plume increasing visual range and indicating wind direction and power. A spiral ramp within the interior brought up mule-loads of fuel and simultaneously provided diagonal bracing to the slender structure. The square sides of the lighthouse were veneered in opulent white marble – a 'weightless' curtain façade such as that identified two millennia later, by architectural historian Henry-Russell Hitchcock, as a key characteristic of the 'International Style'. Sunlight reflected off these orthogonal planes would have provided an additional bearing far out to sea; a sightseeing platform completed the modernity of this wonder of the ancient world.

Each of the contemporary tall buildings reviewed in this book – all built within the last 20 years – incorporates something of the values embodied in that ancient structure. The continuing diversity in skyscraper forms demonstrates that tall-building design has no dominant rationale and remains a protean endeavour. Our definition of tall buildings encompasses both ends of a continuous scale. At one end are concerns of utility: the provision of masts,

observation platforms and transmitters; accommodation compressed by extraordinary land values; foundation conditions; or exotic siting. At the other extreme, it is recognized that tall towers are built with an idealism and a symbolic value; an aspect of the sublime – and are also the embodiment of corporate, global and international power systems.

It will be seen that the technologies applied to these most recent buildings are not governed by any internal logic making them hermetic and inevitable, but are imbued with the values that the skyscrapers are trying to communicate. It is this timelessness and the question of how these mechanisms work that are the interests followed through here: how the technology of building tall structures is influenced by these concerns.

The first high-rise living quarters, the ancient Roman *insulae*, were predominantly utilitarian forms, yet their very name, 'islands', embodies a notion of psychological separation from the immediate surroundings common to many tall buildings. First appearing in the densely populated lower-class Pontine area of Rome, these cheaply built apartment blocks were an early example of economic forces pushing living accommodation upwards. The Augustan Republic was grounded in a special relationship with its urban poor: 'bread and circuses' and these multi-storey chicken coops of rented tenements were two of its manifestations.

Like the Pharos, and so much of ancient masonry technology – the Colosseum and Pont du Gard for instance – the *insulae* comprised tiers of floors: structures of simple arcades repeated upwards. Brick and concrete piers supported arched façades, and vaulted stone floors – levelled with earth or concrete – were developed as a fire-resistant. One by-product of these first tall buildings – so often sited in marginal, marshy land – and of other monumental public works of huge weight, was the first stirrings of foundation theory. Techniques to distribute the weight of buildings into weak substrates and to avoid significant differential settlements, both essential to tall-building design, took their place in the handbooks on construction that had already begun to appear.

Further eastwards, the encounter between the Roman and Persian empires cross-fertilized technologies and organizational systems. Captured westerners and annexed populations were resettled over vast distances, bringing engineering expertise to new environments and materials. East of the Euphrates delta, bricks were sun-dried, but, on the western side, silts in the clay permitted fired bricks to be made. The Persian kings' predilection for vast towering halls was met by using hard-brick technology at unprecedented scales. These *iwan* were masonry extrapolations of the reception tents of the desert peoples. Material and form were combined by coupling tiered superpositions borrowed from Roman construction with parabolic vaults discovered in the plastic processes of bending and plastering reed huts along the great river marshes of the Near East. The resulting technology enabled enclosures more than 30 metres (100 feet) high to be constructed.

Based upon this synthesis of Eastern and Western technologies, tall buildings continued to flourish. The sixth-century Byzantine church, Hagia Sophia – perhaps more towering than tall – used Greek architects together with monolithic elements salvaged from the antique world; its structure, combining the most sophisticated devices of Roman and Eastern building technologies, embodied an engineering-style protorationalism. An efficient, logical enclosure of space within the chosen constructional means was achieved by an iterative process. Without the benefit of any coherent structural theories, the two designers, Isodorus of Miletus and Procopius, grasped and manipulated the structural mechanisms at work simply by observation. Patterns deciphered from the cracking masonry, for example, generated the hierarchies of additive forms.

At the same time, across the oceans, the Amerindians – first the Aztecs, then later the Incas – were building vast artificial hills as temples. Steep, revetted sides were formed with closely keyed limestones and soft granites, bruised into shape using diorite pestles and unimaginable years of manual labour – until first bronze, and then steel, tools were introduced from the eighth century onwards to enable the cutting of harder rocks. However, the social and conceptual strictures of these South American societies seem to have prevented any radical transformation, either of form or of material use, by the introduction of new tool systems.

In medieval Europe masonry construction grew ever upwards, mainly in the form of castle towers and campaniles. In the sphere of weaponry, bows gave way to crossbows – and the geometry of defensive tower and wall consequently developed. Consolidation amongst warring groups also increased the scale and sophistication of siege equipment. Designers responded with ever-heavier construction, and construction plant to handle the heavy blocks was, in turn, transformed. Cranes and lifting equipment were a preoccupation reflected in notebooks of the time.

Gunpowder transformed early fifteenth-century warfare, and the nature of the buildings intended to resist it. The major medieval influence on building construction relevant to the development of tall buildings

Above: The Pharos of Alexandria, c. 290 BC. One of the seven ancient wonders, the structure has many characteristics in common with modern skyscraper designs.

7

was actually the development of descriptive systems and surveying tools to allow the construction of the geometrically laid-out forts and town defences necessary to resist bombardment. These techniques could ensure the accuracy and precise tolerances of construction needed to build high.

The continual warring of the Italian city states, and Venetian resistance to Ottoman expansion, fed the development of gun foundries and, in a side-effect, improved the science of bell-casting. Campanile-dotted across the landscape now called the faithful, signalled threats, marshalled resistance and celebrated the victories of this militaristic society. The new, high-quality castings meant that the bells could be pealed rather than struck with hammers; the movement, in turn, introducing new levels of lateral and dynamic loads right at the top of the towers. Cellular wall sections, ring beams and binders were developed to reinforce the slender brick towers. Extant examples in the Venetian lagoon and, of course, tilting alarmingly at Pisa, exhibit soil/structure interactions akin to buckling instability. Counter measures to this phenomenon centred on improvements to the ancient defensive techniques of piling and consolidating poor ground.

Greek thought, lost to the West after the fall of the Roman Empire, was reintroduced through contact with Arab learning. Islam brought its architectural achievements along with its conquests – foremost among them the minarets: high, slender platforms from which the faithful could be called to their daily religious observance. The spiral ramp at the Great Mosque at Samarra (848–52) perfectly embodies a whole cosmology within its brick construction. The interface of West and East is repeated in the fabric of Seville Cathedral: its bell tower, known as the Giralda, was converted from the minaret left by the retreating Moors.

In northern Europe, the Dark Ages gave way to the era of the cathedral-building campaigns. Stone structures were taken to extraordinary heights, pared down, refined, and decorated with an almost fanatical zeal. The wide communications network across the Christian world, and the techniques used by peripatetic journeymen and stonemasons, allowed technical advances – such as flying buttresses, new vault forms and window traceries – to rapidly disseminate and improve through repeated use. The secrecy of these artisans led to the embodiment of knowledge into formalized patterns of learning. This sometimes arcane application of geometry to building layouts nevertheless offered some control over the scaling of increasingly high structures.

These stone structures reached their apogee in the spire of Ulm Cathedral in southern Germany and the choir at Beauvais Cathedral in northern France. The Ulm spire was an open stone filigree, reducing wind loading and forming a braced tube of impeccable structural efficiency, while the French choir was the outcome of the third attempt to build at such a height. With the balance of vault-spread and confining buttresses finally achieved, the exhausted builders were never able to finish the rest of the church.

Effectively just piles of stones, masonry buildings rely on compressions between the individual blocks for their integrity. Salisbury Cathedral in England incorporated a solid octagonal spire; commenced in 1540 it was for eight centuries the tallest structure in the country. Built on a heavy timber formwork, the Salisbury spire was cleverly prestressed by retaining this centring and reconfiguring it to hang from the spire's finial.

Technical systems develop through a process of innovation, improvement and refinement. So far, these trajectories have

Above: Ulm Cathedral spire, late fourteenth century. The tallest masonry structure ever made. The filigree stonework in the upper levels reduces wind loading.

been presented as gradual processes, progressing through repeated use, mutation and experimentation. The major revolutionary change – and, indeed, the inception of modern structural thinking – originated in the work of Galileo Galilei, who formalized the trend of putting structural design on a rational footing. Structural dimensions would no longer be determined by craft experience and what had worked in the past, but instead would be rationally deduced to meet new environments safely and economically.

Modern rationalization has not been able to bring buildings to a new absolute of refinement in every case: authors such as Jacques Heyman have shown, by back-analysis, that some Gothic constructions, for example, could not have been safely improved upon in any age. Instead, there has been, on the basis of Galileo's advances, a widening willingness to manipulate and explore abstractly. Everyday building is now usually handled with an implicit efficiency. The obverse of these improvements, however, was the monolithic development of received knowledge, binding the use of materials to accepted principles in one encyclopaedic treatment. Enlightenment France led the way in this field, with its Napoleonic codifications of construction – now the model for twenty-first-century globalization's ubiquitous design codes.

It is generally accepted that modern tall-building forms exemplify the forces of industrialization and cultural and social change. The orthodox interpretation of this process is termed 'technical determinism', in which tall tower buildings are seen as solely the inevitable outcome of, and response to, economic and social forces. The version of this story worked through by the architectural critic Sigfried Giedion is now canonical. However, a theory that better explains the current diversity of tower designs is that the path taken was by no means inevitable, but the outcome of contingency and a mix of precedents – some described above. This explanation offers the possibility of almost endless future development, and it is the approach that will be explored in these case studies.

In his book, *Space, Time and Architecture*, Giedion set out a trajectory for the development of the skyscraper: a confluence of technical advances that took place in Chicago and New York in the decades leading up to the beginning of the twentieth century – steel framing, curtain walling, the electric elevator and the telephone. The appearance of these systems coincided with the explosion of economic activity after the American Civil War, which produced national-scale transport and communication systems, the industrialization of farming and manufacture, and the rise of corporate organizations. Plummeting transport costs promoted new concentrations of trade and wealth, and the new railway and telegraph transmitted ideas rapidly. Centralized mill and production facilities began to appear, transforming quality control and the engineer's ability to specify strong and consistent materials.

Within this process, it was undoubtedly the refinement and mass production of iron, a result of the industrialization of war, which gave birth to the tall building as it is known today. Besides its military application, iron would transform machine production and transport, providing plate for steam boilers and tracks for railways. The sheer strength of the material, its forgiving ductility and its reliability in production contributed to its immediate adoption.

Early iron construction used cast and sometimes wrought (hammered) components to make up new building types: warehouses and sheds of all kinds. Reliable tie-rods encouraged large-span openwork roofs. The railway boom relied on rolled rails of uniformly high-quality metal, strong and ductile, readily joined with rivets but forgiving if locally overstressed by bad detailing or workmanship – and this form of the wrought material would be the one adopted for the skyscraper.

The new corporations needed centralized administrations. The telegraph had revolutionized long-distance communication, but it was Bell's telephone of 1876, instantly widespread, that meant people no longer needed to meet face to face – even in the same building. Large office buildings, concentrated on expensive land, began to extrude upwards. Elisha Otis invented the self-braking electric elevator, so that five storeys was no longer the practical maximum for a building's height.

The towns of the American West had been built as a series of timber shanties. The almost-medieval timber frames of the earliest settlers, with their heavy foundation sills and diagonal braces, were almost instantly superseded by sectionalized buildings, prefabricated for catalogue sales or simply clenched up out of lumber from the nearest sawmill. These so-called 'balloon frames' were the first response to the new industrialized production of timber building members: nailed up, light timber studs running the full height of the walls, braced by a plank skin. The system was quickly improved upon, being soon replaced by the 'platform frame', in which the verticals only extended one storey so that walls and floors could be made up as large flat planes to be piled on top of one another and spiked together. Timber-framed houses are still mostly made this way.

Free of preconceptions, the pioneers of skyscraper structures adapted the balloon-frame system to metal. The form was transposed from wood, firstly to iron and later to steel rails – evenly spaced, riveted

together and strengthened with plates. The size and height of such structures was almost limitless, but above five storeys the importance of lateral-load resistance was well recognized. Diagonal braces and rigid knee-joints were freely experimented with. It was not until buildings passed 30 storeys in height, beginning around the 1920s, that other structural concerns became significant.

Chicago had the pioneering outlook, the economic pressures and the solid ground conditions to develop skyscrapers. The Monadnock Building from 1889 by Daniel Burnham and John Root, at 16 storeys, showed that the urge to build high was not dependent on metal technology. Its brick loadbearing structure is Cyclopean – walls half a metre (2 feet) thick at the base – and beautifully proportioned in the fashionable stripped-Egyptian style.

The solutions obtained for iron construction were adapted wholesale to steel when it became a practical substitute. The great improvement in strength and elasticity that the introduction of tiny quantities of carbon and other elements made to iron had been difficult to control and reproduce economically. The new super-material's use was confined to weapons and extreme structural frames, such as clipper-ship hulls, until the military imperative once again intervened. On this occasion, the Crimean War prompted Henry Bessemer, in 1845, to find a cheap and reliable means to mass-produce the material. Steel bridges followed: James Eads' St Louis crossing (1867), in the United States; and the Forth Railway Bridge, by John Fowler and Benjamin Baker, in Britain. The first substantial steel-framed structure was the Tower Building on New York's Broadway by Bradford Gilbert (1889). Foundation systems suitable for the scale of these new structures were, in turn,

Above: The Monadnock Building, Chicago, 1889. The utilitarian form recalling an ancient temple pylon reflects a contemporary enthusiasm for Egyptology.

appropriated from bridge-builders. Not only their methods for carrying large loads, but also their techniques of investigating ground conditions: borings, soundings and trial pits – all essential to economical design – became standard practice in building construction. Cities sited on harbours, river crossings or low-lying areas offered weak soil conditions – alluvia and silts, mostly saturated – on which to build. A four-storey building might bear on the ground below itself with a weight of 2 tonnes per m² (a fifth of a ton per square foot) of plan area. This is within the capacity of most granular soils and clays. At 20 storeys, a load of 10 tonnes per m² (1 ton per square foot) will sink in anything less than the firmest gravel.

Piled foundations – columns within the earth – are an ancient system, and were used in two ways. The earliest examples were fields of posts driven into weak ground to improve it and completed with a rammed-earth capping. Venice was built on this type of artificial ground. The technique was used beneath tall buildings in 1850s North America, and was improved on with the variation called 'sand piling'. In this process, closely spaced holes were made with piles which were then withdrawn, and backfilled with sand – a sophisticated precursor of modern ground-improvement methods. The piling method of most importance to the development of tall buildings was their use individually, either to carry load into the earth by friction along their sides – like giant nails in the ground – or as columns, channelling loads down to a hard-pan or bedrock. Steam power and strong materials meant that new scales of cylinder could be pounded or bored into the ground. The concentrated loads of bridge piers, which were often needed midstream, led to the perfecting of pressure caissons – sealed cylinders, which could be dug out within and which settled under self weight. As in

a diving bell, compressed air kept the surrounding water from getting under the bottom lip of the system. Another alternative followed the introduction of more powerful machinery: the diaphragm, or slurry, wall – a deep concrete-wall structure cast within a trench, capable of carrying great load or of being excavated out to become a basement retaining wall.

Chicago is a city built over a thick stratum of damp, plastic clay, below which is a layer of compacted gravel followed by bedrock. All but its very tallest buildings could be carried in the gravel on grillage foundations: criss-cross mats of steel beams, massively encased in concrete. Manhattan rests on an 'allochthon', or detached sheet, of hard schist rock, but elsewhere in New York ground conditions were not so good and piles and caissons were used, sometimes in combination, to reach adequate bearing strata. The design of the foundations of the Manhattan Life Building addressed, for the first time, the problem of tall buildings in groups. Even with adequate foundations for itself, a tall building will draw down the surrounding ground and affect neighbours. Very deep caissons were used in this case, to avoid damaging adjacent structures.

As frames got bigger – the New York World Building by George B. Post reached 20 storeys in 1889; the Park Row Building, New York, by Robert H. Robertson reached 30 storeys ten years later – their handling became the focus of architectural debate. The outer walls of a building were no longer required to carry all its weight and therefore could be reduced to mere panelling, a 'curtain wall' draping the steel skeleton. Louis Sullivan wrote and spoke about honesty in architecture and, in 1899, produced the Carson Pirie Scott store on the Chicago Loop. Its façade of white terracotta panels, evenly proportioned piers and spandrels surrounding wide windows was patently lightweight, a neutral field across the elevations of the building. This was identified as a significant 'shift point'.

Several other buildings of the period do not fit easily into this treatment. The Reliance Building, Chicago, by Burnham and Root took the idea of a lightweight glazed envelope to its limit, but modelled that envelope with oriels and an exaggerated cornice and spandrels. Burnham was a talented designer: the kind who restlessly explores and experiments, rather than obsessively distils ideas to their essence. Having broken through to a completely modern idiom in the Reliance Building, he then seems to have rejected its seduction. In the same year as the Wright brothers pioneered powered flight, he was drawing and building the world's tallest skyscraper, the Flatiron Building in New York. The curtain walls of this structure, supported at each floor level, were massive stone façades with heavy modelling. The plan of the building took off from the awkward site shape with complete confidence and produced solutions to the unique lateral bracing problems that have proved to be of general use. It became the stereotype of early modern skyscrapers, continually reappearing in cinema films. Over the following 30 years, the skyscraper as a building type grew in scale threefold, through sheer muscle – bigger and bigger frames of the same type culminating in the Empire State Building, inaugurated just as the 1929 stock-market crash and subsequent international economic depression changed the world for ever.

The immense success of these early skyscrapers in Chicago and New York trammelled developments there. Yet significant innovations began to appear elsewhere. Beyond strength and stiffness, the critical structural concern in building has always been fire. The stone-vault linings of medieval cathedrals reduced the incidence of catastrophic timber-roof fires ignited by candles and incense-burning. Mill buildings were constructed in so-called 'fireproof' methods: brick arched floors spanning between wrought-iron beams, partially encased, and all carried on cast-iron columns, which had a reasonable resistance to heat. Under the more intense fire loads of modern buildings something more was needed. Wrought iron and rolled steel quickly give up in temperatures above 600°C ($1,110^{\circ}$F), turning to 'structural pastry', and cold-water shocks from firefighting might induce shattering collapses. Cast-iron columns have better resistance but inferior capacity, and, as uncased standard components, became a common feature of early factories and warehouses.

Linings and fired-earth interlocking casings, such as terracotta, were developed. These were temperamental, however: prone to damage, expensive to fix and difficult to seal properly. Installation, by often unscrupulous contractors, needed careful policing. The Ingalls Office Building of 1904 in Cincinnati, Ohio, at 16 floors, adopted a direct solution to the problem – it was the first office building of notable height to be built in reinforced concrete. Cement, bulked out with stones and strengthened with steel bars, had been introduced as a cheap structural material in the 1860s, with most of its quirks explored and addressed in the French patent systems that predominated up to the turn of the twentieth century. If the covering to the bars was sufficient, it was inherently extremely fireproof. For high construction its chief disadvantage was the long-term shrinkage and creep away from load: a frame made from it shortened appreciably over time. The solution was to use larger, more lightly stressed cross-sections – but the resulting columns occupied more of the hard-won floor

Above: The Reliance Building, Chicago, 1894. The envelope of the building is treated as a weightless screen of glass and terracotta spandrels.

Above: The Flatiron Building, New York, 1899. The heavy stone cladding is suspended off the steel frame at each floor level.

space, floor depths became correspondingly deeper, and the building consequently higher and more expensive than a steel alternative.

As well as perching living spaces ever higher, mechanization also conjured up towers for a variety of purposes. Gustave Eiffel completed his celebrated experiment in wrought iron for the Paris Exhibition of 1889, reaching a height of 300 metres (985 feet). The Eiffel Tower's parabolic taper embodies the logic of the differential equation in its form and a lifetime of practical craft in its construction. Four legs rather than three meant that one of the feet needed gigantic jacks to distribute loads evenly across the filigree, just as a folded bill stabilizes a restaurant table. Thirty years later, the Russian Vladimir Suchov erected a taller tower in Moscow using a quarter of the amount of material. This was not only the outcome of the technological rivalry between the East and the more sophisticated engineering rationale of the West, but also a real economic imperative to reduce material use whatever the labour cost, in the wake of the Stalin-era steel famines. The perfect hyperbolic forms were adopted from naval experiments, where very light observation platforms were needed to keep top-weight down on ironclad ships of poor stability. The forms were also transported wholesale to new applications – like the lightweight, robust landside pylons, both for power transmission and for Marconi's world-revolutionary introduction of radio in 1901. The stirrings of aviation, particularly in the design of the gigantic flight-structures for the first rigid dirigibles – the so-called Zeppelins – focused research onto the handling of very light, braced frameworks and open, thin-walled sections, angles and channels. Together with advances in the understanding of wind pressures and aerodynamics, this work would shape later approaches to tall-building engineering.

The success of these tower initiatives – both skyscrapers and gantries – called for their cultural assimilation. Addressing what they represented and how they were to be understood in turn influenced how their design was to be handled. The output of the Chicago School and its contemporaries in New York has been seen to be more diverse than a convergent historical model would allow. The development of skyscrapers seems always to have continued on the widest front, and this can be observed by looking at competition submissions. Major open architectural competitions are intended to provoke innovation, but simultaneously they serve as snapshots of the range of design thought at any one time. The New York Times Building competition of 1913 or the Chicago Tribune Building competition of 1922, both for the design of newspaper headquarters and consequently of public interest, were subscribed to internationally. For the Midwestern project, North American and European designers displayed a gamut of sensibilities – Modernist through to classicist – all applied to the problem of tall building at that time. Contrasting the 24-year-old Walter Gropius' scheme with that of the winner Raymond Hood, 28, reveals an extreme divergence of form and surface treatments but all are superficial, over common framing regimes.

In literary terms, the skyscraper was easily assimilated as a symbol of the new – especially of the imagined shock and dehumanization of the future. In his book *The Metropolis of Tomorrow* the artist Hugh Ferriss reacted to the modern North American city with sublime images evoking expressionistic awe and limitless scale. The sensibility of an advertising artist was suffused with the ideas and drawing style of the Italian Futurist Antonio Sant'Elia, the draughtsman for an artistic movement celebrating speed and mechanization.

Above: The Eiffel Tower, Paris, 1889. An exhibition building and the first structure to top 300 metres (985 feet). The wrought-iron frame weighs 8,560,000 kgs (9,441 tons).

Rendering techniques using chalk and charcoal replaced wash and lime, to depict limitless surfaces and space rather than closely modelled volumes brought into the light. Coupled with a new urbanism of astounding density, this vision became incorporated into various dystopias. Fritz Lang's film *Metropolis* defined the standard cinematic treatment of urban environments with tall buildings. More recently, the visions of director and draughtsman were coupled in Ridley Scott's *Blade Runner*, presenting ideas of decadence and decay embedded in impersonal buildings, ruins of the mind from the moments of their conception.

At this time, structural analysis techniques kept pace with, rather than drove, development. Assessments of lateral stability were rather simply made, and so-called 'load take-downs' – summations of weight – were generally very conservative. New methods, as they appeared, were applied to the same theories of structural behaviour as those prevalent in the 1880s. The larger manufacturers, as part of their marketing, offered alternative specifications and, within their catalogues, design tables for columns and beams. Based on a variety of theoretical and experimental work, this information was in turn adopted by state and city checking authorities. Different column formulae were adopted in different cities. Carnegie Steel included in their 1893 handbook recommendations for proportioning spread foundations on yielding strata. This was one area where early theory was rather at sea, and beam grillages of the period were consistently underdesigned.

Academic influences gradually regularized the basis of structural analysis. The celebrated teacher Hardy Cross devised a simple and self-checking procedure for designing framed building structures, single-handedly promoting the widespread use

of trabeated frames, columns and beams relying on rigid joints for their stability. Its easy accessibility encouraged uptake at the expense of experiment and diversity. The alternative ways in which a tall building is stabilized were codified. M.S. Ketchum in his book *The Structural Engineers Handbook* (1924) lists four methods of wind bracing: diagonal bracing, knee braces, portal bracing and brackets.

While seemingly irreconcilable attitudes to tall buildings were battling it out for the commission, a radical departure appeared in Europe. The glass skyscraper scheme by Mies van der Rohe, of 1921, had influences clearly traceable to the prevailing German Expressionism. The triangular plan used an enveloping wall, pleated to catch and scatter light. An extraordinary model and complementary charcoal-rendered views depicted a completely transparent skin on a frame of the utmost simplicity, including two structural features that would have a great future: completely flat floor plates without beams, and with columns that were simply circular point-supports (a French-influenced system pioneered ten years earlier by the famous Swiss engineer Robert Maillart); and floor edges cantilevered forward to pick up the completely uninterrupted curtain of the external wall. Its arresting modernity was fully balanced by a simplicity of proportion that was utterly classical.

Other Europeans were theorizing on the possibilities of high-rise living. The journalist Joseph Roth writing in the Berlin press in 1922 was quite clear that the skyscraper represented a new way of living, claiming that the new technology represented 'a sort of return of the evolved human to the primordial forces of nature'. Currents of radical social engineering fuelled ideals for new forms of habitation. The French-Swiss architect Le Corbusier produced a continuous polemic flow of large reinforced flat blocks served by streets in the air, which were intended to free up the ground plane for recreation – a rhetoric tinged with eugenics. Hardened roofs would even simultaneously save the inhabitants from the threat of air attack, as had been the case at Guernica in 1937.

The Second World War demolished much of Europe, and the Marshall Plan confirmed US global expansion. A huge industrial base had been assembled in the United States to produce planes capable of pulverizing the Axis powers, and it soon switched to intercontinental transport, space exploration, and the arms race attendant on the Cold War. Food processing had become industrialized and metals adopted for storage, canning and foil wrapping. Aluminium had been used in the building industry for window frames and doors before the conflict, attractive for its corrosion resistance and longevity, but the post-war boom and the introduction of extruding – squeezing the metal through a pattern to produce long, lightweight and rigid cross-sections – were to make it the predominant material for framing the external envelopes of tall buildings. Fine metal chassis supporting acres of glass transformed the skyscraper. Gordon Bunshaft, chief designer at the US corporate architectural firm, Skidmore, Owings and Merrill, gave a complete expression to the curtain wall – glass on extruded and anodized aluminium – in the Lever House, New York. A neutral net of attenuated transoms and mullions stretched over a classically proportioned vertical office block balanced on a podium of ancillary accommodation.

The architectural diaspora displaced to America from Europe by Nazi persecution had brought with it increasingly refined exercises in the design of tall buildings.

Mies van der Rohe – combining old European origins with a youth of avant-garde experiment and maturity in the United States – refined a style of beautifully detailed and proportioned boxes clad in bronze, which became internationally influential. His Seagram Building in New York and Lake Shore Drive apartments in Chicago became benchmarks of taste and type.

Ever combative and self-promoting, the American architect Frank Lloyd Wright stood his polemical plan for a horizontal expansion of urbanism, Broadacre City, on its head with another proposal – for a 'Mile High tower'. This concrete structure was to be simply enormous, overtopping contemporary buildings thirtyfold and today's tallest building five times over – a lobby of admirers still calls for construction to commence on it. Frank Lloyd Wright always made much of a concept called 'organic' in his work, and the Mile High tower's striking tapered form is indeed structurally suited to the super-high building. Applying structural principles to the parabolic profile of tree trunks, biologists such as Thomas McMahon have shown that the trunks' theoretical buckling limit coincides with the constraints of moisture and nutrient movement and note that it is indeed the height of the tallest redwood tree. Man-made towers share this characteristic; there is a theoretical limitation to their height – strength increasing with height as a square, but weight and wind pressure by the power of three. The theoretical limit is far off, at about 18 kilometres (11 miles) high for current building materials. A more practical boundary, taking into account the imperfections of real construction and the unpredictability of the actual environment, is more like the one mile proposed by Wright.

The Mile High tower's conical form paid scant regard to a more immediate problem

Above: Lever House, New York, 1950. A corporate headquarters. The form is reduced to a beautifully proportioned composition of vertical slab block and podium, the walls to a grid of glass and aluminium.

Above: The Seagram Building, New York, 1954. The tower stands before a wide public plaza. The exposed steel frame is decoration, applied over an inner fireproofed steel frame.

Introduction

of very tall buildings, that of 'lift bunching'. The frailty of the human frame limits the accelerations and decelerations that a vertical transporter can make when rising. The organs of the human body effectively hang within a frame unrestrained against such movement. As buildings get higher and the number of their floors increases, the number of stops that can be serviced in a reasonable time becomes limited. Really tall buildings, perhaps those of more than 60 storeys, have lower floors congested with the lift provisions necessary just to reach the upper areas. Sky lobbies can help, in which very fast lifts take people high up without stopping, to transfer points whence a shorter lift journey in a slower system reaches their destination. Movement into and around such buildings, however, cannot be so easily resolved. In one of the tallest buildings in the world, the Sears Tower in Chicago, occupants can stand in line for up to two hours just to depart at the end of each day.

The last 40 years has seen towers grow exponentially in size. The appropriate structural design of super-towers, those over 100 storeys, became a research topic shaped by the work of Myron Goldsmith, a structural engineer within the integrated consultancy of Skidmore, Owings and Merrill, whose architects, structural and environmental engineers and cost consultants collaborate under one roof. Together with his pupil Fazlar Khan and a group of Illinois Institute of Technology (IIT) doctorate students, Goldsmith's stated objective was to reduce material use. Seeking optimum weight designs, his team came up with the 'mega-frame' concept for the tall tower. The seminal John Hancock Center of 1969 on the Chicago lakeshore was the result. Here 100 floors are set within a massively scaled cross-braced frame of principal members, which carry lighter subframes, floors and columns. The system

is inherently robust, and may be matched with other organizing principles; storey-height plant floors, sky lobbies or fire separations can be arranged behind belt trusses, girding the tower at vertical intervals.

The Sears Tower of 1973 embodies another concept, the bundled tube. One of nature's strategies, typically seen in the closely packed cross-section of the bamboo stem, this idea prefigures the large-structure concept of the mega-frame: grouping a number of subframes to interact and create a very stiff whole. The inventor and visionary Richard Buckminster Fuller's challenge, 'How much does your building weigh?', is a clarion call taken up by more than one contemporary architect. The weight of steel used per square metre of usable floor area is a simple benchmark by which to test a design. The 148 kg/m² (30 pounds/square foot) for the Hancock Center compares favourably with the simpler trabeated structure of the similarly sized World Trade Center, weighing in at 244 kg/m² (49 pounds/square foot). The Sears Tower used 188 kg (37.5 pounds) of steel for each square metre of area it provided. The measure is, however, a crude one. Overriding linear comparison is the general tendency for weight to reduce as height increases to 30 storeys, and then climb more steeply again beyond this for taller buildings. Total embodied energy, the real expenditure needed to put the structure in place, may be distorted by intricate details and complexity in assembly. The large diagonals expressed on the John Hancock's elevations, for example, significantly complicate its cladding system.

New ways of making tall buildings do not have quite the same glamour as the resolution of an innovative structural form, but probably contribute more to overall economy in construction. The German idea of open, 'landscaped offices', egalitarian and

Above: The John Hancock Center, Chicago, 1969. The 'megaframe' concept of engineer Myron Goldsmith is worked out in a tower of powerful simplicity.

16

encouraging exchange, dispelled the cellular office and typing-pool divide of the standard American model in calling for open flexible space, well lit by windows. The resultant layout standard, enclosed central circulation core, and fire refuge surrounded by wide-span floors bearing on a hull of perimeter structure, promoted the construction pattern of a rapidly assembled core, perhaps slip-formed in reinforced concrete, becoming the bracing stem of a light steel frame, prefabricated and rapidly erected around the aligning centre. Stem and casing, once locked together, become capable of resisting the wind loads of the clad building, and earthquake forces if necessary. More recently, the hull component of such configurations has been recast as 'super-columns', concentrating capacity into massive built-up members to leave floors and façades more flexible for architectural manipulation.

An alternative organization is to set vertical circulation outside the main floor plates. Confined sites are well addressed by this strategy and the plan efficiencies, the ratios of usable to total floor space, are exceptionally high. The accommodation and circulation systems go up separately, not casting a critical path across one another. Bracing moves to the outside of the envelope – expensive, but capable of joining with the visible vertical elements of circulation and service risers in the expression of the building.

Within the phenomenon of the global spread of tall buildings since the Second World War, the response or indifference of their design to local environments and cultures is a telling aspect of their reception. The Lever House model, with ever-slicker envelope, has been spread across the Western world and around the Pacific Rim. Le Corbusier's scheme for the United Nations Headquarters in New York

demonstrated his mastery of the idiom. In his mission to continually reinvent architecture, his end-wall treatment of that building presaged his subsequent influential variation: the development of a sophisticated treatment of large expansive, modelled façades held between formal end-pieces. In reinforced concrete these motifs came to predominate in South America, becoming an almost indigenous idiom through the work of Brazilian architect Oscar Niemeyer and others.

In Europe, Gio Ponti's Pirelli Tower in Milan, its plan manipulated to make the building faceted in the light, was much copied. The idea that a single encompassing design approach could be applied to any artefact, from kitchen utensils to cars, had been extended to skyscrapers. German examples show strong influence from across the Atlantic. The steel barons of the Ruhr built their new Düsseldorf headquarters, the Thyssen House, as a well-proportioned ranking of slab blocks. An echelon of floor plates is linked by intervening circulation spaces: another arrangement that has remained in use, despite a relatively inefficient use of space.

France and Britain's predisposition, by contrast, has not been to build high. Paris and London came late and reluctantly to the seemingly inexorable worldwide spread of tall building. As part of the microwave communications network and civil defence communication system, London's GPO Tower was constructed as a hardened stem of reinforced concrete, its Brutalist handling unconcealed under a functional tiering of accommodation. The nearby Centre Point, by architect Richard Seifert and engineer Willi Frischmann, is a precast reinforced-concrete structure of the utmost sophistication. Highly modelled units, integrating beam and column, were prefabricated and brought together to form a pierced casing. Poured concrete then tied the assembly together into a robust whole, free of internal columns. Architect and engineer subsequently collaborated on the Nat West Tower, the tallest building in the City of London. A concrete core carries huge brackets of concrete above the narrow alleyways and courts of the City's ancient street plan. A light steel frame springs from this elevated platform, braced back to the rigid lift and riser shafts.

One more example from that building boom illustrates further construction ingenuity. Hearts of Oak House is a modestly scaled building on the Euston Road in north London. Its central core is conventional concrete, but the walls and floors are then suspended from a top gantry housing plant and lift motors. Hangers cannot buckle like columns, and so the outer frame is lighter and more efficient. Such assemblies require care in construction, as disproportionate settlements can accumulate as work proceeds.

Diversity and experimentation were not confined to Europe. In North America, as well as the working through of the first generation of super-towers, several smaller initiatives proved of lasting consequence. Bertrand Goldberg produced the most exquisite pair of residential towers in the Chicago Loop district. Marina Towers comprised ranks of flats fronted with heavily modelled precast balconies, set high above helical in-situ concrete parking ramps. The stark imagery of this 'corn on the cob' building is recalled in several of the novelist J.G. Ballard's stories, to denote a certain kind of modern high-rise living.

The Knights of Columbus Building (1965–1969) by Roche & Dinkeloo offered a unique departure. A large-scaled structural armature here gives shape to a legible circulation system. The large open plaza extending beneath the building is a recurrent device of the architects, first used in the practice's Ford Foundation in New York, a design in which the modern office atrium building sprung into fully fledged form. At the Knights of Columbus Building the narrow floor plates preferred by agents and lessees are arranged around an enclosed space, which becomes the heart and orientating centre of the building. Fire strategies followed up recent innovations, to make it possible to open out floors into these volumes without fear of flames or smoke spreading uncontrollably. More recently, atria have become the areas on which environmental engineers have concentrated to improve the natural conditioning of buildings, airflows and daylighting provisions.

Louis Kahn, working in the 1960s with his long-time collaborator, the engineer August Kommandant, took up the ideas of Buckminster Fuller to produce some outlandish schemes and megastructures intended for a new urbanism. Vast structural armatures, threaded with services, were intended to carry reconfigurable accommodation. In Japan, these ideas were extended by a group of architects called the Metabolists and realized in a few examples, such as Kurokawa's Nakagin Capsule Tower where the notion of dwelling unit as cell within an agglomeration is literally achieved.

Alongside these experiments with new form went a steady refinement of existing means. Possibly the slickest skyscraper ever built, I.M. Pei's 1976 Hancock Tower in Boston, Massachusetts, is a triangular shard with sheer elevations of mirror glass literally glued in place. Toughened glass panels, heat-processed to improve strength and robustness, were stuck to metal subframes with 'structural' mastic, without mechanical fixings, bolts or lugs. Unfortunately, this daring innovation came to grief. Firstly its

Above: Marina Towers, Chicago, 1960. A perfect example of precast construction combined with in-situ framing and a complete lifestyle embodied in concrete.

Above: Knights of Columbus, New Haven, Connecticut, 1965. An extraordinary excursion into a new rationale for a corporate headquarters.

neighbours sued successfully when their air-conditioning bills soared owing to an excess of reflected light; then the building was nicknamed 'the plywood scraper', and the surrounding streets closed when storey-height panes of glass began to fall out of the upper levels. The technique was persevered with, however, and is now one of the most reliable cladding systems in widespread use.

Over the last 30 years, the American engineer Leslie Robertson has worked through a trajectory of structural refinement, reducing weight, and simplifying bracing systems and jointing methods in tall-tower frames. Amongst his many significant tall-building designs are the World Trade Center towers, at the time of their construction fêted as an exercise in lightness and dispersed structuring. The twin towers' flimsy fire cladding, permitted in the harbour area of New York City, proved inadequate to the extremity of an unthinkable terrorist attack. Another extraordinary event in Robertson's lifetime of achievement was his involvement in the saga surrounding the Citicorp Tower (1977), a 59-storey tower, also in New York. The building was complete and occupied when the engineer for the project, William Le Messurier, was alerted, by a phone call from a student, as to a possible mode of collapse that had been overlooked. With a vast building fully occupied in a densely populated city-centre area, and with an approaching hurricane predicted, the story of the subsequent actions of Le Messurier as original designer and Robertson as one of the checking engineers makes an essential case study in professionalism for aspiring engineers. The role of the media, especially *The New York Times*, in exaggerating and destabilizing an already fraught situation is also fascinating to those in practice.

The public reception of the Citicorp incident, almost an eagerness to prejudge the situation, indicated that attitudes to the problems of tall-building design and engineering were largely conditioned. The 1974 disaster movie *The Towering Inferno* played on people's received knowledge of the very few large tall-building fires that had occurred. Relying on fairly accurate technical understanding, the story is set in a building swollen so large that circulation is difficult. The extensive provisions of risers, both wet and dry, that have to be incorporated in such a building to bring means of defence to all potential fire sites became locations for the adventure. Escape provisions, refuges and protected routes, structural fire-resistance, and the ability of a building to remain stable long enough for any foreseeable fire to be brought under control, are all in the tale.

Other popular reflections of an underlying unease include J.G. Ballard's 1975 novel *High Rise*, which proposes a group psychosis as one outcome of multi-storey living. Less speculative research into the human consequences of building high remains, predictably, inconclusive and the phenomenon, in any case, is now global. The tendency for tower designs worldwide to settle into the cycle of North American styling is counteracted by the response of designers to ideas that forms should reflect their environment. Different places call forth different preoccupations. Structurally, two widely varying sets of imposed loads – seismic forces and wind loads – are the predominant influence on built form.

In certain parts of the world the importance of lateral loadings on tall buildings is compounded severalfold by the risk of earthquakes. Regular small shocks must be considered as well as anticipating a major event. Along the margins of the tectonic plates, on which the continents drift, the rock frets and grinds. Shudders and stutters create explosions of energy that vibrate outwards, propagating themselves

Above: Nakagin Capsule Tower, Tokyo, 1972. Standardized modules for single business workers are mounted on a pair of towers and secured with only four bolts each.

Above: World Trade Center, New York, 1966. The efficient steel-framed 'hull and core' structures succumbed to an appalling terrorist attack on 11 September, 2001.

as waves across the surface. As well as lifting and cracking the carpet of the earth's crust, these waves stretch and compress the ground's surface horizontally – and tall buildings can be waved back and forth like palm fronds. Unfortunately, most high buildings vibrate at about the same frequency as the incoming ground waves, resonating and absorbing energy like tuning forks, and the resulting inertial forces are difficult to contain. Building frames can become very heavy to counteract this, and towers in seismic areas have a characteristically hefty appearance. Alternatively, the natural resistance to vibration within all structures – 'damping', or the ability to shed energy through internal friction – can be enhanced by mechanical systems, to reduce overall structural weight and retain visual lightness.

Tropical weather systems can create very high winds. The hurricanes rising in the Caribbean swirl across the southeastern seaboard of the United States, restrict the size of high rises and give them a curious thickened look: columns and spandrels become muscular and monolithic. In the South China Sea, convection cells grow and mature in the typhoon season. Storms bring winds slamming into obstructions with a force equivalent to the weight carried by a typical office floor. The stretched glass façades of the banks and condominiums of the Pacific Rim cities must resist loads equal to all those filing cabinets and desks, but applied sideways in sudden bursts. Glass panes are smaller, and window frames and sunshades heavier than in northern climes.

Recent competitions continue to chart the diversity characterizing high-rise design. The 1982 competition for a new headquarters building for the bioscience company Humana pitted contestants well

chosen from a range of architectural thought against each other. The winning building, by Michael Graves, is the epitome of US 'high post-Modernism'. Norman Foster's exercise in a rational integration of engineering and operations shaped his practice's subsequent output. The competition for a new development at Ground Zero, New York, on the site of the destroyed World Trade Center was probably skewed by political undertones and histrionics, but, again generated a spectrum of initiatives.

Currently, the dominant theme in tall-tower design is the improvement of environmental-control systems. Energy use has always been profligate in such buildings: a 100-storey tower might burn as much energy as a 12-hectare (30-acre) city block. Once it is accepted that simply using air-conditioning systems in all climates, from tropical to subarctic, is not sustainable, then buildings must take on strategies to relate themselves to their immediate surroundings and microclimate. Their envelopes need to be insulating, to keep at bay swings in the outside temperature. Daylight is a human need, but at variance with the general requirement to prevent sunlight overheating interiors. Ventilation is used to bring some of the thermal requirement to occupants.

Much ingenuity has focused on the skin of each building. Appropriating depth at the expense of floor, external walls have become buffer zones of variable permeability, mediating energy transfers in and out of the building. At a larger scale, built forms are being adjusted to incorporate open spaces and sky gardens – extensions of the dedicated storey, formerly plant space and now given over to communal use. In larger units, occupants tend to stay on site for longer periods

Above: Humana Building. Louisville, Kentucky, 1985. Post-Modernism required its buildings to be decorated with very overt iconography.

combining work and leisure activities, and a hierarchy of space and amenity supports this behaviour pattern.

The scale and height of tall buildings affect wind environments locally, and for several decades downdraughts and local funnelling effects have been studied using wind-tunnel testing to mitigate adverse conditions at ground level. In the last decade, this work has extended to airflows at higher level and within atria or open storeys, which might be used to naturally ventilate the building. Setting up airflows that are fully controllable is difficult. Computational fluid dynamics, the digital modelling of patterns of air movement developed for aircraft design, provides an economical tool to investigate options. The complexity of the atmosphere's behaviour makes a model-test of the final design essential. The architect Jan Kaplicky of Future Systems has explored the idea of harnessing the focusing shape of buildings to obtain energy from the wind. His project, Zed, proposes an autarkic building, shaped to enhance an integral wind turbine. The building's external envelope is loaded with photovoltaic cells and the building is constructed as a minimum-weight frame, taking full advantage of its double-curved form and set on shaped foundations to touch the ground lightly.

Skyscrapers in preparation at the time of writing seem to be extending the quest for sustainability and habitability, unquestion-ingly accepting the validity of such towers as a sound use of the world's resources.

Less intellectually inconsistent is the straightforward striving for the world's 'next tallest tower'. Kowloon Station, by the Australian architects Denton Corker Marshall – currently 'on the drawing board' – is a contender for the world's tallest building. Set over a mass-transit railway terminal in Hong Kong, this super-high tower becomes intimately associated with a transport interchange directly below. One building is a mixed development with a balanced provision of amenities. Traditionally, residential units have been placed as high as possible to exploit the view; in this project, the desire to keep the structure efficient in the face of anticipated buffeting from typhoons ensured that offices are set above residential units. The city's storm alarm will have sent everyone home, and the empty upper floors can be allowed to sway without disquieting anyone. The lower floors are occupied by a luxury hotel remote from, but fully linked into, the city and its air-conditioned retail malls.

Daniel Libeskind's proposal for the World Trade Center site in New York is suitably ambitious in scale. The design is inherently flexible, to incorporate the many changes and inclusions that the consultation processes with the numerous users seem to generate. An openwork megastructure, based on a braced tube, will hold various functions, and a wind chimney is proposed to distribute cooling and ventilating air throughout the form. A spiritual emphasis on light, in this case artificial illumination, means that full advantage of the building's surface is being exploited, using a veneer of photovoltaic cells to generate power for the complex.

The 29 case studies which follow are chosen from the output of the last decade from all over the world, to reinforce the model of design progress adopted here. There is a pool of influences from which particular samples are drawn as a mixture, rather than as points on a continuous trajectory or network. Each example is analysed as a composition of ideas, and a particular technical interest is highlighted in each case.

Above: Project Zed, London, 1995. Experiments exploring the sustainable use of resources in tall towers are beginning to influ-ence mainstream commercial design.

BUILDING **WING TOWER**
LOCATION **GLASGOW, UK, 1999**
ARCHITECT **RICHARD HORDEN**
ENGINEER **BURO HAPPOLD**

An open design competition for a 'Millennium Tower' held in Glasgow in 1992 yielded 353 entries. The winning proposal, published in an excellent catalogue recording a huge range of designs, was for a slender, sightseeing platform that tracked the prevailing wind. The whole 200-tonne tower rotates on a massive base bearing.

References to the city's heritage as a seafaring, shipbuilding and manufacturing centre are combined in the scheme with a very modern technological idealism and drive for regeneration. The design proposition makes a direct connection between nature and a city shaped by nature.

The architect Richard Horden and his collaborator, aerodynamicist Peter Heppell, are both very successful competitive sailors and their submission documentation tracks an aerodynamic design development guided by the intuitive feel displayed by those regularly engaging with the elements. The designer's principles include a fastidious attention to using materials sparingly and correctly and to the placement of buildings

with infinite care – 'to touch the ground lightly'. Form, devoid of preconceptions, arises directly from these preoccupations. In the case of a tower, a streamlined stem that leaves a minimal wake in the surrounding airflow is the lightest possible free-standing shaft. Windage is reduced and the possibility of wake instabilities avoided. The central stairwell and lift guides are faired and airflows are channelled and smoothed on either side by vertical fins. The three-part system is braced by secondary tubes to form a vertical, space-frame truss capable of resisting lateral loads and twists.

The imperative to reduce weight was adhered to throughout the design process. The Eiffel Tower uses up a profligate quantity of steel: 8.56 million kg (9441 tonnes) – more than 28 tonnes for each metre (9.6 tons/foot) of its height. Vladimir Suchov, building transmission towers during the steel famines under Stalin in the Soviet Union, managed to get down to a quarter of this figure: 6.3 tonnes/metre (2.2 tons/foot). This is a realistic benchmark for modern

Above: The Wing Tower rotates on a base bearing to face the prevailing wind. The stem and buttressing fins are coupled to make a minimum-weight structure.

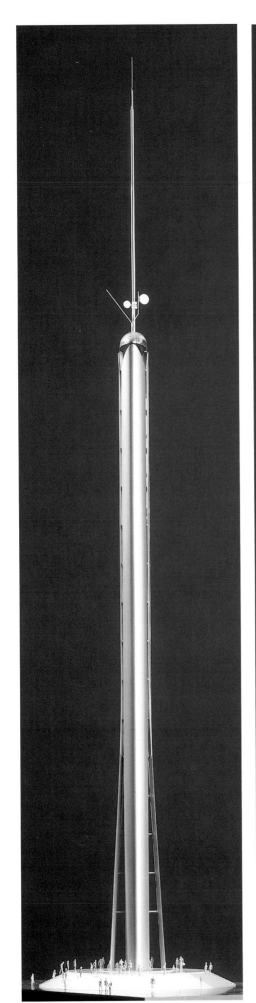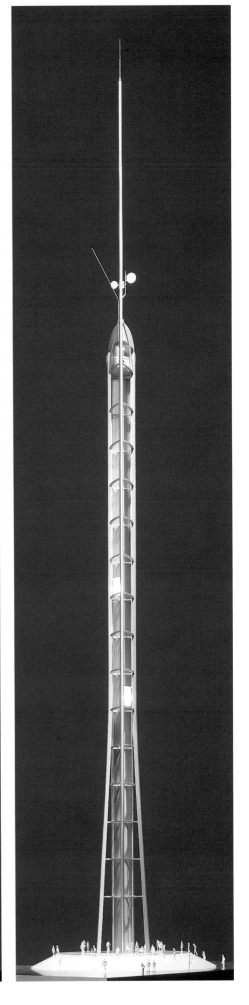

Above: The spiral staircase to the viewing platform is streamlined within a fairing. Fins form slots to guide airflows smoothly over the surfaces and into a steady wake behind the tower.

25

construction; a solid option for the Wing Tower weighed in at approximately 10,000 kg/metre height(3.4 tons/foot). In the final openwork scheme this structural weight is halved and the windage on the structure's side, a possibility if the mechanism were to stick, is minimized.

The observation platform was designed as a giant cockpit canopy for 40 people sheltering on a lower open deck. A balanced pair of lifts, ferrying ten people at a time up and down for half-hour visits was arranged on the system centreline to avoid swinging as the whole tower turns. As built the lifts are self-propelled climbing cars, streamlined and arranged with conjoining doors for evacuating people without drama during a breakdown. The simple climbing mechanism, a rack and pinion system with the motor carried with each lift car, does not intrude on the lines of the tower.

The movement of the structure in the wind is carefully engineered. The lateral acceleration of the top deck that can be considered comfortable – 50 milligees (thousandths of the force of gravity) – is about the level experienced in a London Underground train. On the six days or so a year when this threshold is exceeded the platform is closed to visitors.

In the design development an active system of trim tabs was proposed to further reduce the structure's response to buffeting by the wind. With the introduction of two small fins activated mechanically, and set in the vertical slots formed by the main structural booms, turbulence could have been sensed, computed and responded to, just as the flaps of a modern airliner work actively to minimize roll and pitch in flight. However, the weight-saving of the system's implementation could not justify its complexity.

Great pains have been taken about the way the building meets the ground plane. One of the winning considerations noted in the judges' report was the handling of the installation within the surrounding cityscape, and the potential for public activities. The engineering of the revolving mechanism uses proven technologies but they are applied at a tour-de-force scale. Tower cranes, swinging freely in the wind at the end of the working day, can be seen in most cities. Their slewing bearings, loadbearing pivots between mast and jib, are small cousins to the giant turret rings of the battleships that were once built on Glasgow's River Clyde. The moving part of the tower is about two-thirds the weight of the revolving gun platforms once fitted at the nearby dockyards. The same pattern of support and mechanism is used in both systems.

The weight of the tower is carried down onto a central bearing set in the bottom of a concrete pit behind the old dock wall nearby. At ground level an outer rim of roller bearings, set on rubber dampers to reduce vibration, forms a turntable. Overturning of the tower is taken out by the opposing forces that develop across these spaced-out supports. The foundation pit is a circular, concrete, diaphragm wall. A trench was dug from ground level and backfilled with concrete to make a sealed enclosure of ground. This was then dug out and the base plugged. This lined hole distributes the bearing forces into the weak surrounding ground. The mechanism is left open for viewing like the engine room of a ship.

The Wing Tower is a unique experiment, the precursor of structural forms that will one day not only meet their environment head-on but, instead of dumb resistance, will also adapt and respond to the flow of forces across our Earth.

Right: The form of the tower is developed around a consistent set of principles rigorously applied. The least disturbance is offered to the passing airstream. Sections are prefabricated and rapidly mounted.

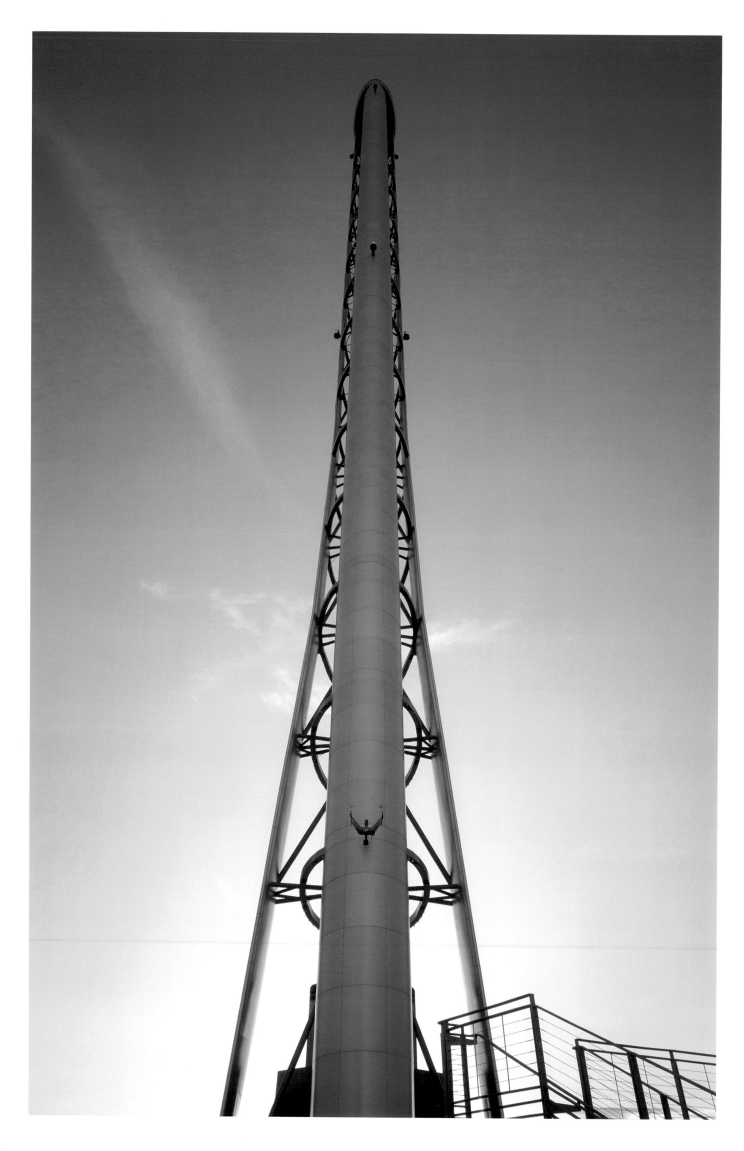

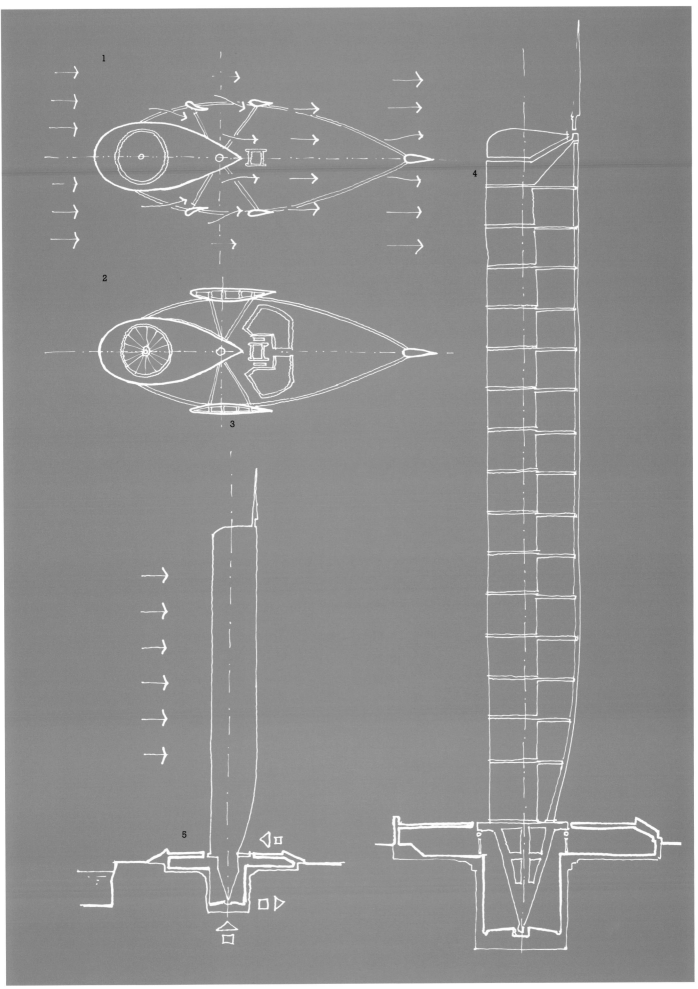

Left: The vertical circulation – stairs and lift guides – is parallel sided. The efficiency of the vertical cantilever is improved by splaying the outer fins onto the perimeter of the supporting bearing.

1. Trim tabs are incorporated into the slot between the central body and outer fins. These flaps were to be adjustable in pitch and controlled automatically, sensing and then compensating for fluctuations in the wind.

2. Access to the observation platform is by a pair of climber lifts, each a cabin and motor running on rack and pinion. The cars interconnect in case one breaks down.

3. The outer fins of the tower are connected to the core to act in unison as a braced girder. The fins step down in size and divide in two as the tower rises and the bending forces tail off.

4. The tower is prefabricated in transportable sections and then stacked using a mobile crane. The observation platform canopy is sized to the practical limit of a frameless acrylic moulding.

5. The weight of the tower rests on a central pivot-bearing set in the base of a cylindrical cofferdam. A slewing bearing above ground level couples with this bottom pin to resist lateral loads.

BUILDING SWISS RE HEADQUARTERS
LOCATION LONDON, UK, 2002
ARCHITECT FOSTER AND PARTNERS
ENGINEER ARUP

This is a speculative office development intended to be let on the open market. It is also the tallest building to be erected in the City of London for 25 years. The striking silhouette records how a design process that draws together the ideas of disparate thinkers and inventors, identifying their essences and then reconciling these with tested methods to m ake a new whole, can create a radical-looking building while remaining within an essentially conservative remit. If there is experiment in the design it is made only if an alternative route reverting to more traditional means can be retained.

The design advertises its commitment to sustainability, starting from the notion that new building forms will appear when resource use is approached in a more responsible way. The streamlined form may appear to refer to earlier experiments in the expressionist style of architecture, and indeed a whole range of arbitrary icons are tabulated by the architects themselves as visual references. However, a purely pragmatic justification is also applicable, based on three advantages. The building shape has been tuned to shelter the surroundings rather than aggravate downdraughts, particularly important in the ancient street-and-alley pattern of the City of London. With smooth airflows, heat

losses across the tower's surface are reduced. (This may not be of particular relevance to a building operating almost entirely on energy gains from occupants and equipment). Wind-pressure coefficients are reduced, so there is a reduction in the pressure on the building. Opening lights can be made at higher, windier levels than would otherwise be possible. In order to explore these ideas about air flows the architects employed the services engineers who had earlier worked through a thought experiment with architects Future Systems for a building whose streamlined form aimed to minimize heat loss, structural weight and disruption at ground level, to achieve a self-sufficient building. Practical forms that gave benefits in all these areas were modelled and tested. In addition, the cross-flows on the tapering façades were exploited to provide pressure differentials across segmental lightwells cut through the floors in a helical pattern. It was shown that the building could be naturally ventilated for up to 40 per cent of the year. Space was left in the building to retreat into full year-round mechanical handling if necessary.

The structural form adopted to achieve the double-curved shape is efficient, with a long background of development. A hull structure is theoretically the most efficient

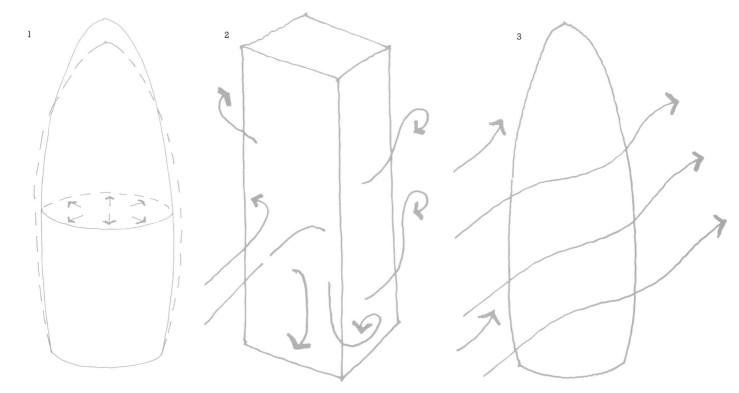

1. As construction proceeds the building frame shortens and barrels out under its own weight. Component dimensions are pre-adjusted to compensate for this.

2. Airflows around bluff objects break up into eddies and downdraughts. Tall square buildings can cause gusting at street level.

3. Streamlining a building reduces wind pressures and hence structural weight. Low-level wind speeds are not accelerated and it is claimed that heat losses are reduced.

Above: The entasis of the glass tower reflects light in a unique way. The double Saturn-ring gantry rails allows the window-cleaning crane to reach far out.

31

tower-form possible, sharing the organic response of bamboo to minimal material use. Here a steel frame, comprising a central braced core – containing lifts, risers and stairs – from which radial steel beams span onto a perimeter of columns, carries floor plates of lightweight concrete acting compositely with profiled metal soffits and supporting beams. This version of a hull-and-core structure takes 36 outer columns and forms them into a self-bracing diagonal grid structure similar to the form explored in the practice's Humana Building competition entry 20 years earlier – and taken originally from a Barnes Wallis airframe design. The barrel shape needs tying to control spreading and perimeter hoops are incorporated at each floor level. Advances in computer-aided manufacture, which have filtered through to the steel-fabrication industry over the last decade, have made it efficient to draw, analyse and make non-standard components, marked and delivered in a just-in-time sequence of erection.

The top of the building becomes something other than the traditional termination of a tower; instead of the now-familiar antennae array, huge cornice, etherealizing crown or decorated penthouse there is a smooth transition curve into the apex. The specialist fabricators Wunderberg were taken on to complete this inevitable nose-cone. The diminishing panels of cladding are tiered elegantly, terminating in a plexiglas shell reminiscent of an aviator's astrodome.

The building touches the ground with immense sophistication, a trait of Foster buildings. Spaces around and under it are intimate and natural. Helical atria are a neat inflection of the circular organization; an economic alternative to the sky gardens of the practice's Frankfurt Commerzbank. Segmental cuts into the volume of the 'gherkin' shape let in air and light. Each floor void is rotated 5 degrees from the one below to create a spiral volume – a simple, elegant architectural trope yielding beautiful space.

The shifting hull-profile conjures up some clever structural detailing to accommodate the changing angles of members. The junctions of the circular columns are simple flanges and the ties are pinned straps. Adjustment is carefully built in to compensate for tolerancing issues. The market remains geared to structural steelwork fabricated to low accuracies and any improvements are inordinately expensive. Accordingly, the convoluted floor shapes made cutting standard deck-panels to shape expensive and wasteful.

Tall buildings change shape as they are assembled and their weight increases and

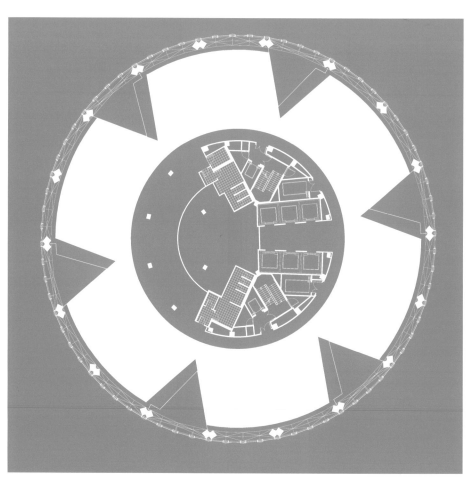

Above: The office floors are compartmentalized and visually interconnected through segmental atria spiralling up the building. The offset of each floor precludes vertigo.

Above: The Cartesian repetition of standard joints is replaced by complicated computer controlled fabrications, delivered in sequence and fitted just as easily into a coordinated whole.

Above: The dispersed
framing of the building
reduces the visual weight
of the form, and the structure touches the ground
lightly forming a loggia
all around its perimeter.

is redistributed during construction. These effects need special consideration in towers of more than 30 storeys high. Predicting and compensating for movement in this building is more difficult than in conventional perpendicular frames, as vertical settlements combine with horizontal spreading of the thickening waist. The computer calculates this movement so that nodes can be positioned, initially offset in space. The growing structure deflects into its final desired position only as work proceeds. This process, so-called 'precambering', is fraught with difficulty. The elasticity of the base material is invariant but a number of factors contribute to make an accurate estimate of movement difficult. The rolled members are not exactly the cross-section specified. Joints do not behave as modelled. Additional gussets, end-plates, fish plates and stiffeners all add to the resilience of the structure. Prototype mock-ups are made to test the practicality and safety of assembling large components at height, but these units are seldom loaded and assessed for actual flexibility. Physical tests can be used to re-calibrate preliminary computer models to improve accuracy. The actual behaviour of the building as it rises yields more information, from which refined adjustments can be made to the work ahead.

The twin-skin façade is made up of a conventional fully sealed outer skin of double-glazed lozenge and triangular-shaped panels. A small angular displacement across each mullion shapes the envelope onto the curved surface of the building. An inner lining of single-glazed sliding doors, openable only for maintenance, completes a perimeter void containing adjustable sunshades. This space buffers the interior thermally and can be ventilated independently to remove heat build-up. Outside air can also be drawn in through the spandrels, conditioned, and blown directly down from the suspended ceilings where needed. The planning requirement to maintain the appearance of the building in the round compromises its rationale. North-and south-facing walls are given the same treatment, maintaining a beautiful axial symmetry at the expense of optimum energy use.

The structural frame of the building is fully enclosed and insulated by the envelope, the best way of controlling temperature changes that could distort the main frame. Some of the building's expressiveness is lost; it looked clearer as a pure frame and the transparent outer wall is marred by the heavy cased members passing through.

One of the most interesting facets of the project has been the interaction of architects and letting agents. The building varies from 50 metres (165 feet) in diameter at the base, to 57 metres (187 feet) at its widest point, to 25 metres (82 feet) across its highest floor. This entasis gives a more pronounced shaping than the figures might suggest, but the changing areas of floor plate have not been well received by the market. If agents work on the assumption that there is a perfect floor-plate depth and area to be recommended to clients it follows that many of the floors in this building will not match the ideal. Variety of spatial experience and the Piranesian perspectives of the atria count for little. Several of the floor voids are being closed over, a provision that was fully allowed for in the original design.

Above: The top floors of the building are treated differently from the main shaft. A geodesic glass and steel dome floods a series of mezzanines with light while fully exploiting the view.

BUILDING   LONDON BRIDGE TOWER
LOCATION   LONDON, UK, IN PROGRESS
ARCHITECT RENZO PIANO BUILDING
           WORKSHOP/BROADWAY
           MALYAN
ENGINEER   ARUP

London is a world city, and world cities need tall buildings. The truth of this axiom is tested in the context of achieving ever-increasing densities of occupation, and of using resources, built fabric and transportation in efficient and, hopefully, sustainable ways.

Britain's capital is also an old city, a tablet erased and reinscribed many times. Building tall in the City and West End has traditionally been resisted as unnecessary, and contrary to the nature of those places. A whole complex of issues, amongst which aspiration is not unimportant, is forcing a re-examination of this tacit policy.

There are several technical responses to the political forces at work, and they must resolve contradictory impulses. On the one hand, building in and around the square mile of the City is controlled under a warped umbrella of sight lines to St Paul's Cathedral – the centrepiece of Sir Christopher Wren's Renaissance plan for London. Additionally, new buildings must not to be visible from within the baileys (outer courtyards) of the Tower of London. Opposing this is the architect's ideal of building high and compact. On first seeing Manhattan in 1924, the only criticism Le Corbusier, the influential French-Swiss architect, had to make was that the skyscrapers were not packed tightly enough. This idea is now convention, resurfacing in the notion of a 'city core' of extremely high density.

Another way of handling high rise is to exile it outwards. In London, the old docklands have been transformed into the Canary Wharf conglomeration where towers, stunted by the glide path of the City Airport, make a second centre of gravity in the East End. The place is busy, pristine and anodyne.

A third option is to land a megatower in one piece: a building of mixed use, big enough to contain all the beneficial functions of a small town. London Bridge City – a proposal for a development in Southwark, just south of the river at the point of the original Thames crossing – is such a project. Space for 7,000 people – a veritable township – will include apartments, shops, offices, restaurants, leisure facilities, and even a museum, all within a single armature. The site sits over one of the busiest transport interchanges in England, the southern gateway to London.

The aim is to erect the tallest building in Europe. The pyramidal form is supposed to reduce overshadowing. It certainly resolves the problem of lift-crowding at lower levels. The very tall structure can be served by a staged bank of 39 lifts, without sky lobbies, and 12 escalators criss-crossing the wide low-level spaces. The steel structure buttresses itself naturally. The apex of a pyramid is a difficult volume to occupy efficiently, and it becomes less stable structurally as one approaches the tip. Aerodynamic effects, building shape interacting with wind to produce vibration, are an additional concern. The disadvantages of adopting this form are neatly turned by the designer, by making the finial a giant radiator structure. Looking across any city early in the morning, one sees the earth's resources steaming off into the atmosphere from concealed cooling towers. Here, shedding heat elegantly is made into a design issue.

The tower's inclined planes and all-glass cladding are intended to reflect and scatter light. Though it would be a fabulous expense, it is claimed that white glass will be used throughout so that the prism will appear to recede. The prism is intended to recede into the sky. England's maritime heritage is also pressed into service to support the form, which is intended be reminiscent of the masts and spars once lining the river, and is described by the architect as a 'shard of glass'. Presentations

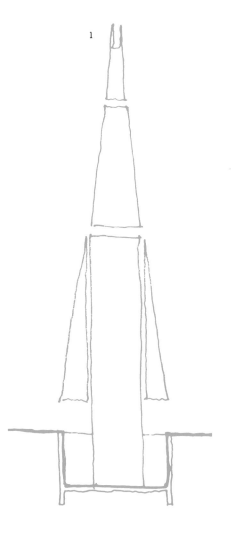

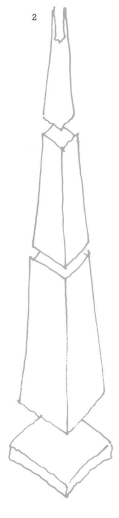

Left: Like a Caspar David Friedrich painting the sloping surfaces of the glass shard will catch a continually changing spectra of blues and greens from the sky.

1. The pyramidal form subdivides into a composition of simple structural systems. A deep basement and raft foundation supports a central core with sloping side frames.

2. The angled surfaces of the building reflect skylight rather than surrounding buildings. White glass (unadulterated by iron impurities) will retain the clarity of reflected light.

3. The tower is divided into a mixture of uses. The narrow apex is cleverly appropriated as a heat-ejecting stack. The sides of the building overhang the public realm below.

Following page: The transport interchange beneath the tower will be spacious and top lit. The main load-bearing structure will be dispersed into a forest of slender columns.

for major projects nowadays all seem to incorporate such metaphors in order to hook the media. However, claiming that the spire will be 'disappearing in the air like a Sixteenth-century pinnacle', conjuring up memories of C.R. Cockerell's famous watercolour capriccio of Wren's and Hawksmoor's London churches, might represent the nadir of this practice.

Much of the debate surrounding the project revolves around the issue of the public realm. The swamping effect that such large developments can have upon their surroundings are well recorded from examples in the Pacific Rim cities. This project incorporates an acreage of public space at ground level that is associated with the upgrading of the dilapidated transport termini beneath it. Halfway up the 66 storeys of the tower, a triple-height piazza space is formed full-width to bring visitors to the heart of the building. Public viewing

galleries and restaurants occupy the highest habitable levels.

There is something of the stalking horse about this project: the intention to trigger an open policy debate on tall buildings in London. It is a practical proposal, and is supported by many concerned with London's future, including the current mayor. The tower is at such a scale that it is prone to simpler more fundamental concerns than most building proposals. It may be a relatively 'safe' intervention in the city, but if there was an unforeseeable consequence what would its magnitude be? How can a high-quality project by a 'signature' architect be safeguarded against financial erosion, and brought to an uncompromised conclusion? Technical means and design expertise are well prepared to deliver these projects. The protocols needed to govern their procurement must match these facilities.

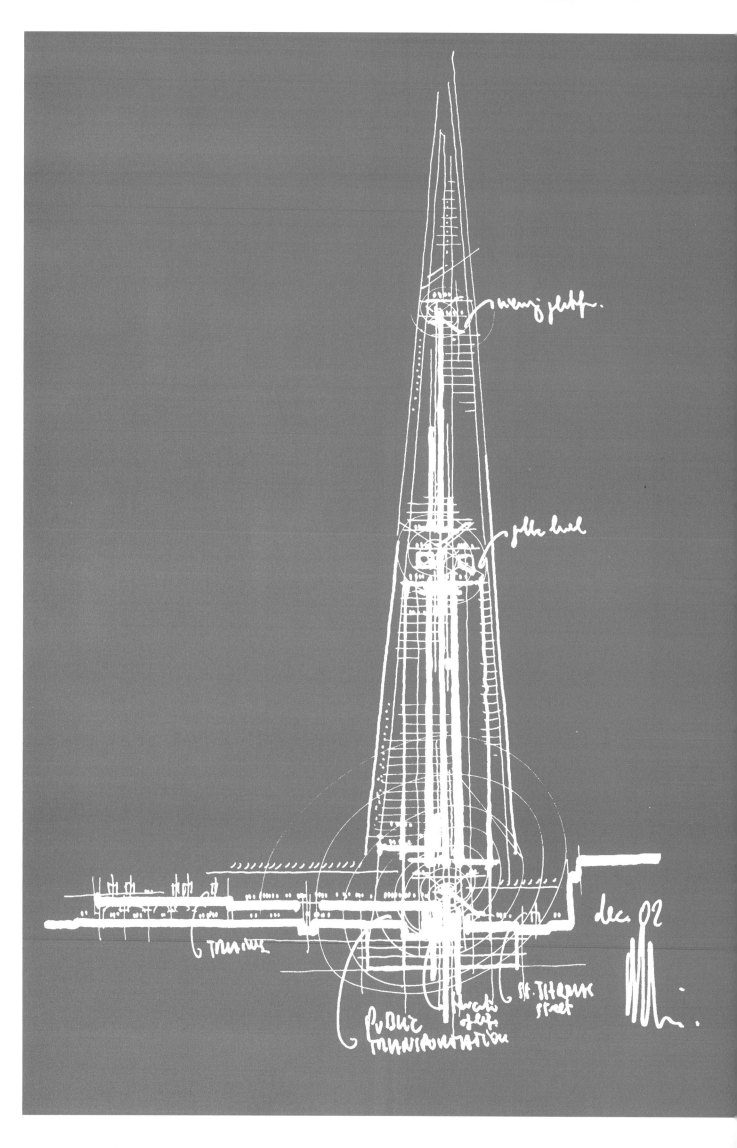

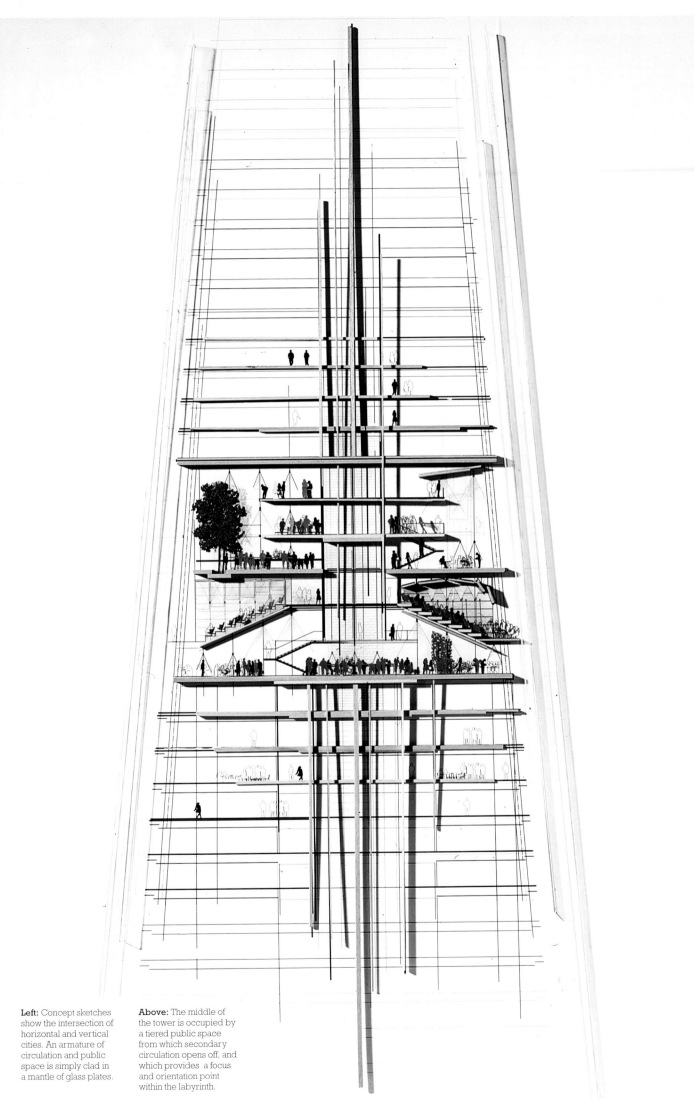

Left: Concept sketches show the intersection of horizontal and vertical cities. An armature of circulation and public space is simply clad in a mantle of glass plates.

Above: The middle of the tower is occupied by a tiered public space from which secondary circulation opens off, and which provides a focus and orientation point within the labyrinth.

BUILDING **GRAND UNION BUILDING**
LOCATION **LONDON, UK, 2003**
ARCHITECT **RICHARD ROGERS PARTNERSHIP**
ENGINEER **PELL FRISCHMANN**

The theorist Cedric Price proposed a new way of building: assemblages of elements with clearly designated roles and inbuilt capacity for reconfiguration and extension. He built little, but influenced a generation of architects through his teaching and example. Starting from the celebrated competition win for the Centre Pompidou 30 years ago, the architect for London's new Grand Union Building has systematically explored and expanded these ideas. This latest project stands on a long trajectory of design development, a steady reduction to essentials, and a continual review of design ideas as they work out in practice. This mixed-use development attempts to be the perfect rational design-response to its type and location. The utilitarian chain of design decisions is leavened by a careful attention to proportion, light and space, and architectural concerns are not overlooked.

Paddington Basin is currently the largest designated regeneration area in London, a gateway to the West End of the city. On an intersection of ageing transport systems – railway, canal and urban motorway – this dilapidated industrial area is being replaced by a waterscape of office, residential, retail and leisureaccommodation. The basin terminating the Grand Union Canal becomes the major public space, and Grand Union Building the centrepiece of the development.

The very large, high-density building is divided into a series of floor plates, staggered on plan and packed around atria for daylighting. These 'served areas' are accessed and interlinked by cores: 'servant areas' containing ancillary spaces, lifts and stairs. The stepped massing of the blocks addresses planning issues of scale, mediating between motorway and neighbourhood high road. Indeed, in the course of this project the tower height and massing changed significantly, without compromising the scheme. The rooftops are all exploited as gardens and green space for residents and office workers.

The hierarchy of articulated elements makes the building's organization legible.

Above: A highly differentiated massing of accommodation and circulation allows planning requirements limiting height and bulk to be readily addressed.

Right: Flexible armatures of structure and circulation provide a variegated backdrop to the redevelopment of an entire city quarter.

Circulation spaces and lift cars are fully glazed, linking inside and outside. Passers-by and occupants alike are able to see and be seen, engaging with the building. Expensive and largely opaque firewalls, separating occupied space and escape routes, are concentrated into the junctions between block and core. The building's parts are freely adjusted to occupy and reflect the irregularities of the site. Together with the vertical towers topped with service capsules, this makes for a picturesque composition.

Building structure and services are treated conceptually as distinct components of the whole. The tower frame perfectly meshes with the space-diagram. Floor-plate width is set by daylight requirements, length by escape distances to protected shafts in case of fire. The resultant rectangular decks are supported around their perimeters by circular columns of minimum section. Floor depth is determined by the cross span. This allows room for relatively deep spandrel beams on the long sides, which, when connected to the columns, provide adequate bracing for the tower on its long axis. Cross-bracing is only required on the

short end-walls. In this scheme, diagonals are expressed outside to become a scaling device adding grain to the façade treatment. The V-configuration puts the elements into tension, so that slender high-strength ties can be used, reducing visual obstruction. The full-height glass walls have external shading where necessary, producing another, finer, level of filigree.

At ground level large, brightly coloured air intakes shaped like ships' ventilators animate the public terracing. Bright colour is carried up the service risers of each core. This treatment is almost vestigial, an ironic comment on earlier experiments where services were rigorously held outside the building envelope and colour-coded like an industrial plant. This 'over-articulation' proved expensive in weatherproofing and maintenance, so a more relaxed approach to enclosure is taken here. It is this intertextuality with previous RRP projects that gives the design such interest and richness within its simplicity.

Beaubourg, the Centre Pompidou, was a flexible machine for housing culture, with floors that were to be movable and external services to be worked over and rerouted. It

was followed by London's Lloyd's Registry Building, a bespoke headquarters building expressing responsiveness – at considerable expense. The Lloyd's building showed how efficiently a difficult site could be occupied, how structure could be integrated into form and how a transparent stair-tower could be efficiently made. Speculative offices at Wood Street took the client request for a completely glazed envelope, and produced a reliable combination of coated double-glazing and external louvres. All these innovations, adjusted and improved, appear on the Grand Union Building. More than the other examples discussed in this book, the project offers, through its elimination of the unessential, a programme to develop a genuinely justifiable skyscraper.

The motif of oversized cleaning cranes employed here refers back to earlier, un-realized schemes for mutable buildings, compartments moving incessantly within an armature. There is a conceptual shift here, the operational idea being reappropriated a as design tool. The building cannot actually move, but the set of articulated elements offer a design system of great flexibility, responsive to diversity.

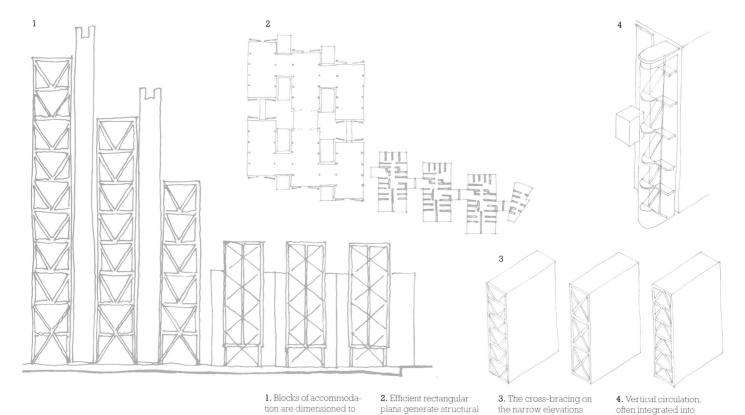

1. Blocks of accommodation are dimensioned to allow natural daylight and cross-ventilation throughout. Lifts and stairs act as vertical accents.

2. Efficient rectangular plans generate structural frames stiff enough to resist wind loads without bracing on the long sides and with only cross-bracing on the short ends.

3. The cross-bracing on the narrow elevations of the blocks can be configured in several ways. The inward slopes adopted mobilize the full weight of the building to resist overturning.

4. Vertical circulation, often integrated into the lateral bracing elements of towers, are here treated as very lightweight substructures filling in peripheral areas.

Above: Occupants moving within the glazed staircases and lifts animate and humanize the building façades. Motor rooms form classically proportioned terminations to the transparent shafts.

Following page: A kit of parts – three-storey office blocks, flat levels, vertical circulation towers and roof gardens – is composed into a balanced elevation of trinities.

45

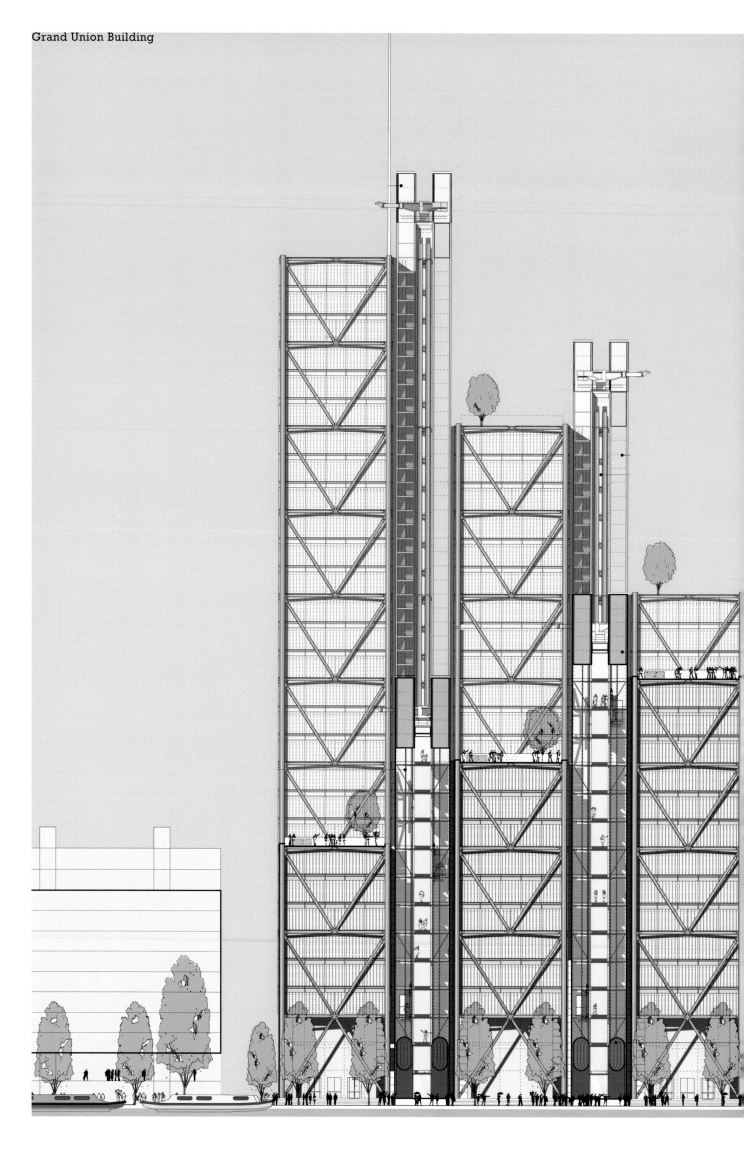

Grand Union Building

BUILDING   **HERON TOWER**
LOCATION   **LONDON, UK, 2006**
ARCHITECT **KOHN PEDERSEN FOX**
ENGINEER   **ARUP**

The City of London has traditionally resisted tall buildings. The townscape, institutions and unique sociology of the square mile have militated against high-rise development. Acknowledging world competition – and the towers rising to the east at Canary Wharf – clients, architects and planners are now returning to the consideration of appropriate high-rise development in Britain's main financial centre.

The 36 floors of this speculative office development defer to Tower 42 (formerly the Nat West Tower), currently London's tallest building, by six storeys. The form reflects social concerns. It is carefully integrated into its surroundings and closely reflects the characteristics of its market. The opportunity to consider the overall sustainability of urban development was incorporated into the design development.

Sited on the line of the old Roman wall, just where the *via principalia* of the original camp once set off northwards, the building is on the periphery of the 'City cluster', a planning concept that aims to concentrate high-rise development. Monolithic central-core topologies were rejected by the designers in favour of offset vertical circulation. As well as producing better floor space, each elevation could then be treated

differently. Bland curtain-walling, hermetic and faceless, was eschewed in favour of legibility and animation. From its position on a notional boundary and as a 'gateway' marker, each face of the building responds to the characteristics of the district facing it, and to the overall orientation to daylight and prevailing winds.

In order to offer the highest quality of work environment, psychological and behavioural cues are accepted into the design. The bulk of the building is broken down into 11 three- storey 'villages'. These social units of about 300 people group around north-facing atria, which draw the floors into a common space and which can serve as trading floors, libraries, exhibition areas or casual meeting spaces. Views are set up into the heart of the building and out over the city. The distribution of space, and planned flexibility, meet the profile of potential lettings. Small-scale service industries such as lawyers, accountants, and media and e-commerce companies can be accommodated. Two tenants per floor is practical. Structural capacity is provided for stairs and bridges to be added, to link and organize larger units of space.

The grain of the City is compact, and the planning of the building's ground floor is

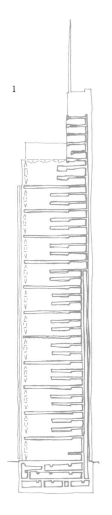

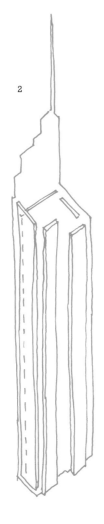

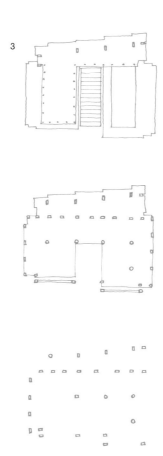

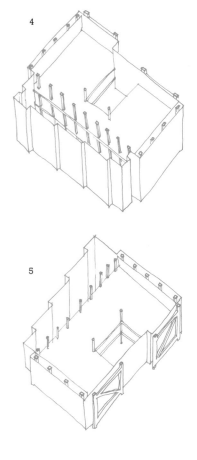

1. The building is organized into three-storey units of space opening onto south-facing atria.

2. The hull structure is interrupted by the atria windows. The south-side structure is brought outside the building envelope, reinforced and cross-braced as part of the building's expression.

3. Circulation and enclosed spaces are set along the north side of the building. The ground floor opens public routes across the site.

4. The façade varies with each aspect. A double-skin façade on the east and west buffers the main offices. A single skin encloses the north-side core and a glazed façade opens southwards.

5. The external structure must be fully insulated so that external temperature changes do not rack the building frame as elements expand or contract.

Right: The building's bulk is broken down by the massing of components – circulation, structure and external blinds – and by the subdivision of accommodation into three-storey units.

intended to reinforce the existing pattern. The surroundings to the tower base are pedestrianized. A three-storey-high arcade along the west side – made roomy enough for substantial planting – is offered as a 'public village', and a new plaza to the north frames views of the visually swamped St Boltoph's Church. A panoramic lift links the ground plane directly to a rooftop restaurant and bar.

The scheme's approach to resource use follows an interpretation of 'urban renaissance' principles, criteria intended to encourage appropriate development. The site sits well within London's transport strategy, close to bus termini, and two railway and ten Underground stations. Computerized daylighting studies showed the optimum atrium shape and floor plans. The building's south side is completely shielded from heat gain by the core, and the east and west sides are triple-glazed with coated glass and automatic glare and heat-gain blinds incorporated within sealed units.

The core structure itself is unusually big, stepping back efficiently as the lift provisions diminish up the building. Double-deck lifts reduce volume wasted in shafts. There is sufficient space at every level for localized plant to provide full air-conditioning, so that each floor can be run independently. A heat-recovery system operates on the ventilation provided to each 'village'. Straightforward suspended ceilings and raised floors, with their low levels of customization, ensure that the work areas can be quickly fitted out with a wide range of identities and data-service provision with the minimum of waste.

The scheme's structure follows its form closely. Conventional steel framing and composite floors in both the main tower and core areas are adjusted to underscore the building's organization. On the north face the stacked 'villages' are defined by external bracing forming triangulated panels three storeys high. This elevation is split by the central atrium spaces. The perimeter

structure, continuous and concealed within the curtain walling around the rest of envelope, becomes two tall pylons of framing set outside the enclosure. The external expression of structure in tall buildings sets up potential movement problems in elements exposed to the cold or to strong sunlight. In this project, outside components are insulated within a fine jointed casing. The effortless way in which the frame appears to pass from behind the core into the double skins on east and west sides then outside the north elevation is a well-handled integration of structure and envelope.

The building does not attempt to be an extreme departure or to express its innovation outlandishly. There is a close integration of environmental engineering, structure, form and organization. A well-balanced composition is achieved, as is a very modest feel to a large building, which will allow it to settle into, and contribute to, the established fabric of London.

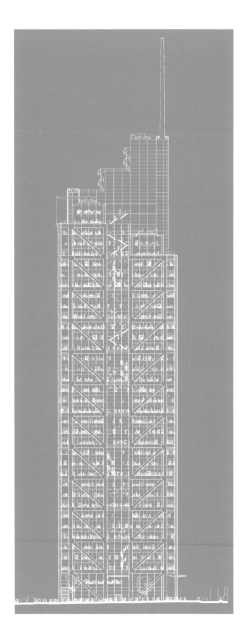

Above: The south façade is given depth by the layering of structure and envelope protected by brise-soleil and by shadows cast off the external framing.

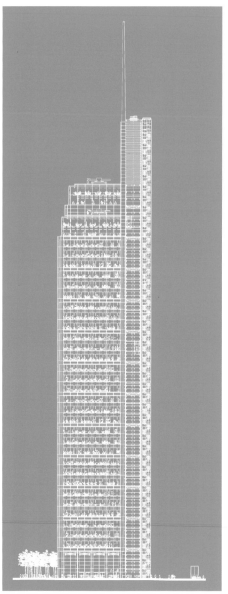

Above: The north façade is carefully proportioned with occupants visible as they move up and down stairs and lifts to and from conference rooms.

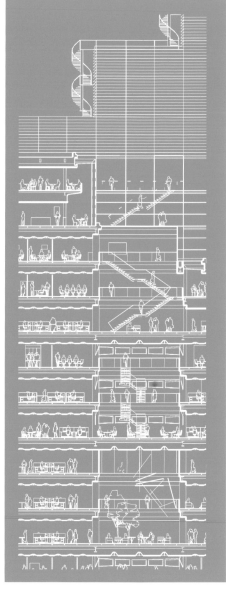

Above: The building section allows floors to be interconnected with feature stairs or opened out into trading spaces, auditoria or landscaped rest areas.

Above: Advantage is taken of the views over London to install a glass pavilion and public gallery. A true penthouse of steel and glass stands on the roof terrace.

Above: From along London Wall – the line of the old Roman fortification – the elevation is developed with a vertical emphasis terminating in a communications finial.

51

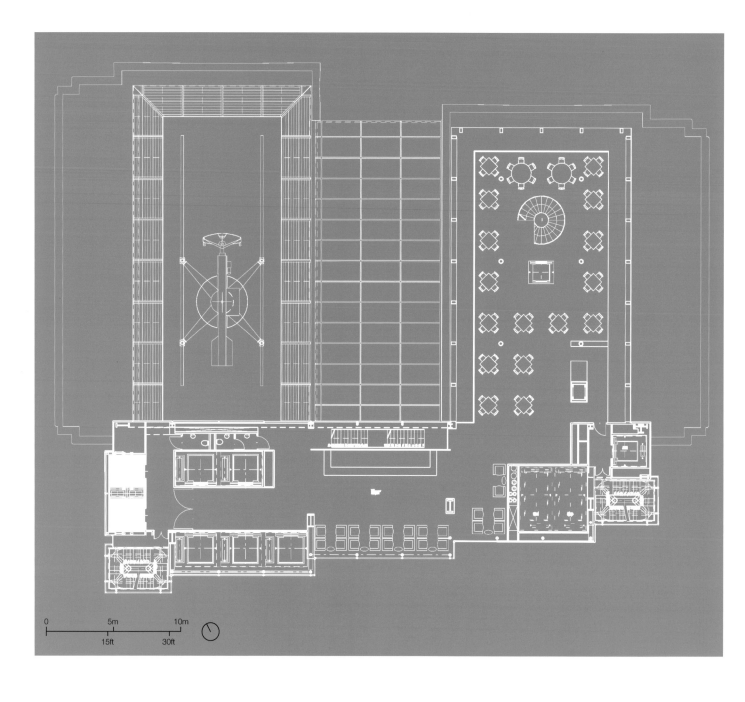

0   5m   10m
|----|----|
  15ft   30ft

Above: Ground-level and topmost floors occupy the elementary frame of the tower with secondary structures: open-plan observation decks or enclosed loading bays.

Right: The offset core zone, peripheral structure and south-side atria permit a variety of space arrangements: open-plan office land-scape to cellular offices.

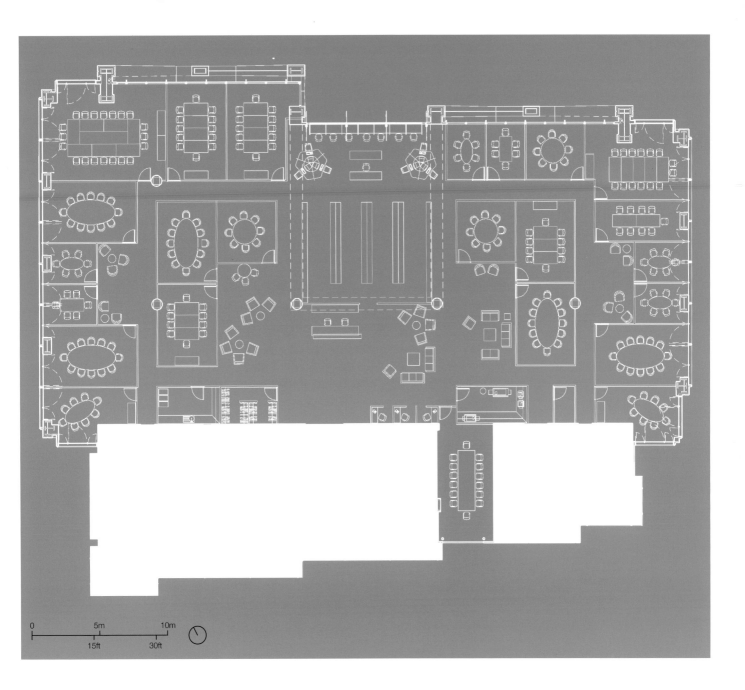

0 5m 10m
15ft 30ft

BUILDING **THE SPIRE OF DUBLIN**
LOCATION **DUBLIN, IRELAND, 2003**
ARCHITECT **IAN RITCHIE ARCHITECTS**
ENGINEER **ARUP**

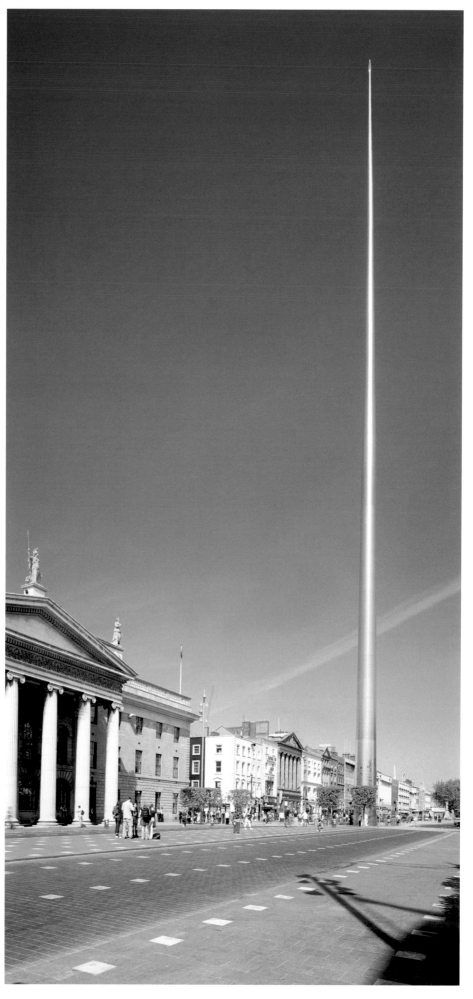

Above: A platonic solid brought into the light. The purest structure would have been a parabolic taper melding into the ground; instead the attenuated cone appears weightless and without scale.

This Millennium monument forms the centrepiece of extensive urban renewal in Dublin. The topography of the Irish capital, low and spreading at the mouth of the River Liffey, is exploited with a soaring needle refined to the utmost simplicity. Despite being the winner of an international competition the scheme only obtained planning permission after a drawn-out public inquiry and appeal. It is the protection of the Georgian city's distinctive skyline, with tall building strictly controlled, that ensures the spire's effect. It relies on its singularity in the surroundings. Catching the shifting light of a north European maritime city is the purpose of its elemental taper and subtle surface.

As well as celebrating the city's third millennium the installation occupies a significant location: it sits alongside the General Post Office, the Republicans' headquarters, appropriated during the Easter Uprising of 1916, and on the site of Nelson's Pillar, an imperialist symbol dating back to 1808 which was destroyed by the IRA in 1966.

The subtlety of historical and cultural reference is paralleled by a deeply considered response to technical change and development. The seamless, hollow shard counter-intuits the monolithic timelessness of standing stones and obelisks. The columned monuments of the Georgian age, their neo-classical proportions relying on fretting between the keyed blocks of the cylindrical shaft to resist alternating wind loads, become an exactly proportioned metal tube, bolted and protected by a mechanical damping system.

A precise taper of 1 in 40 on a height of 120 metres (390 feet) allows the engineer to generate a minimum set of practical dimensions, an exact reference to the artefact's environment. A 3-metre (10-foot) base width narrows to 150 millimetres (6 inches) in diameter at the vertex.

Just as an ancient obelisk is all of a piece – alien and hard material – so the modern high-tech example applies contemporary metallurgy as part of its expression. The high-grade stainless steel used throughout, resistant to the marine salt and traffic exhaust combined in the Dublin air, is detailed to avoid the crevices and stress-raising corners where corrosion can set in. The building is to last 120 years. Instead of incised graphics on its shaft the whole wand is evenly finished by shot-peening, a military specification in which the metal surface is hammered to a dull sheen under a hail of fired shot. First a pounding of cold iron pellets kneads the base material down, contaminating its alloy so that a second process of cracked-glass-bead abrading cleans the surface back to a fine sheen. The original purpose of the process was to eliminate microcracking from the surface of highly stressed components, postponing the onset of metal fatigue under cyclic loading. It is characteristic of the mast's designer to reveal the lyrical potential within the technology, almost as if it were a craft. The finish is easy to repair on site, almost uniquely among metal finishes and vital to achieving invisible site-jointing.

The shaft is fabricated as a series of frustra, or truncated cones, joined by bolted flange joints. This form of joint is the simplest connection to make between tubes and its structural behaviour is well understood following research prompted by North Sea exploration. Lower sections are in 35-millimetre (1⅜-inch)-thick plate, rolled in quarters and then joined by full-penetration butt welds made smooth and consistent with

Above: Base detail. A machined plate mediates between spire and ground plane. The graphic clarity of the drawing transposes directly into the built form.

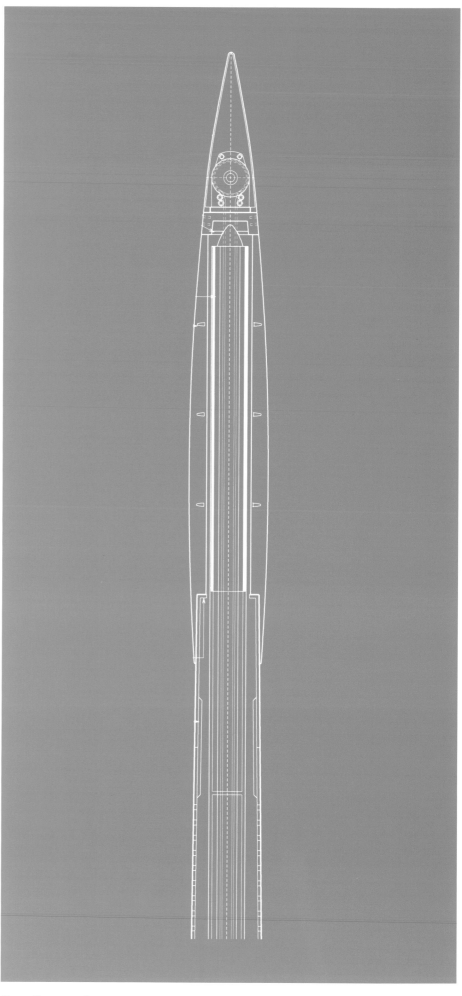

Above: The apex navigation light is mounted on a retractable spline so that all maintenance can be carried out from within the structure.

automated machinery. The narrower upper stages are pressed to shape in thinner plate to avoid cracking and weld distortion. As part of the lighting strategy these components are pierced with a close pattern of holes. Lamps within shine up onto the punched rims, which are graded to create a rising illumination.

Access – both at construction stage to set the flange joints, then later on to adjust dampers, inspect and relamp – is rigorously thought through, becoming an important generator of the design. A beautifully refined access ladder leads up the centre of the tower to various platform levels. The apex warning lights are arranged on a slide system to retract down the centreline of the hollow spire, for maintenance within the safety of the enclosure.

The thin superstructure is founded on a ring of bored piles anchored down to the underlying bedrock and earthed against lightning. The pile cap incorporates an

underground access chamber of reinforced concrete, hiding the electric switchboards. The junction of shaft and ground is acknowledged by a collar of cast bronze decorated with an incised spiral pattern doubling as an effective anti-slip surface.

The development of monoplanes in the First World War rapidly revealed the problems associated with slender flexible structures in airstreams. Instabilities, classical flutter, stall flutter, wake flutter, galloping, vortex shedding and Dutch roll all amount to a dangerous build-up of energy where the onset of movement in the solid affects the surrounding airflow, locking into an escalating pattern. The shape of the object can be adjusted to push the onset of such effects beyond anticipated airspeeds but, just as other considerations set aerofoil shapes, so the preferred form of the tapered needle requires another strategy: the addition

of damping. A structure's natural propensity to dissipate energy when forced into motion through friction across its joints and heating between the stretched molecules of the fabric is enhanced by adding artificially generated counterforces or passive shock-absorbers.

The Dublin Spire relies on a passive system of internal pendulum dampers hung on wires and moving within viscous oil. The resonances of the structure were estimated by computer, and weights set to swing at these frequencies and draw energy off. Assumptions had to be made about the real structure – joint stiffness and precise material behaviour – and the mechanical system was made readily accessible and adjustable. Once installed the response of the actual structure could be checked by instrumentation and the dampers fine-tuned to respond to the real conditions, a process essential to their effectiveness.

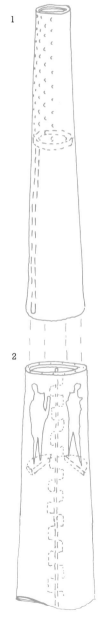

1. The spire is assembled from fully prefabricated sections sized for road transportation and brought, fully cabled and fitted out, to be lifted in tiers onto prepared foundations.

2. Site connections are made through flanged connections match-fabricated at works, which can be bolted up by riggers working from within the safety of the structure's enclosure.

3. The free-standing wand vibrates in a series of increasingly complicated waveforms. Closely spaced natural frequencies mean that the higher modes influence the structure's real behaviour.

4. Circular sections are prone to wind excitation from 'vortex shedding' – eddys breaking away rhythmically – and 'galloping' – lateral forces induced by air-flows across surfaces.

5. Excessive movement due to wind excitation is prevented by fine-tuned dampers. Pendulum weights are adjusted to swing with the natural frequencies of the structure.

BUILDING	TOUR SANS FIN
LOCATION	PARIS, FRANCE, UNBUILT
ARCHITECT	ATELIER JEAN NOUVEL
ENGINEER	ARUP

Eiffel's tower for the Paris Exhibition of 1889 met with a great deal of opposition and vituperation. Zola and Maupassant were amongst 300 petitioners calling for the supposedly temporary exhibit to be cancelled, the latter claiming it to be the reason for his self-imposed exile. This deep-seated ambivalence to tall building in the capital, and indeed anywhere in France, has endured. Partly as an aesthetic reaction to industrialization, the very necessity of tower building to the Modernist project is put into question.

The 'Tour sans Fin' project, still unbuilt after a decade of debate, offered an architectural solution to this resentment. As a Millennium project at the end of a long line of 'Grand Projets' – government

building initiatives intended to reinvigorate Paris – the skyscraper was to be sited at La Tête Défense. This area west of the centre is set on a vast urban structure extended from Haussmann's celebrated town-planning interventions of the 1860s. Here, since the 1960s, the city's authorities have consistently applied Modernist principles of town planning to their waves of development: Le Corbusier's ideas of zoning and grade separation materialized as director Jean-Luc Godard's *Alphaville*. After suffering during the 1970s oil crisis, the area's blight was addressed with the construction of a new shopping centre, housing and the Grand Arch of 1989.

City planners had formulated a

Above: Sited within the Tête Défense area of Paris, the Tour sans Fin appropriates the effects of atmospheric perspective to evaporate into the horizon.

development strategy of towers in clusters on the ring road, away from the old centre. Roger Saubot's Maine-Montparnasse, at 203 metres (666 feet) the tallest building in France, had been ill received in 1973. The new building at the transport nexus of La Défense was intended to be more than twice as high. As a visual hinge it would unite the disparate elements; as an almost classical element, it would become a campanile adjacent to the Grand Arch.

The design focuses all its technology on making a beautiful object. The tower was to be the slenderest in the world. Stretching from ground to sky its substance was to dematerialize as it rose: the embodiment of a spiritual connection between earth and air,

the almost inevitable outcome of this particular architect confronting the tall-building problem. This single stroke of simplicity was met by the directness of the technical proposals. The framing is entirely peripheral. Uninterrupted circular floor-plates span onto perimeter walls. Like a Saturn V rocket, the structure is staged. A slip-formed base of pierced concrete walls becomes a steel hull-frame dissolving into a diaphanous glass top. Engineering efficiency is maintained in the parallel shaft of this rival to the Eiffel Tower, diminishing within its fabric rather than in form as it ascends. Grey granite cladding gives way to softer limestone and then glass, screen-printed in a graded tone; the whole sheathing a

Above: The concrete tubular structure gives way to a steel frame and then a glass sheathing as it rises. The layering of envelope and structure, and the building's cylindrical form, etherealize its outline.

geological section extracted up onto the earth's surface. The building is firmly grounded, disappearing into a pit 25 metres (80 feet) deep and with a diameter just a few metres wider than the tower.

The cylindrical structure splits vertically down each side of the building, with the halves reconnected with cross-bracing. Up these clefts run banks of lifts. Floors adjacent to the high-speed lifts on the north elevation could be hollowed out to make atria: interconnecting volumes between sky lobbies. These spaces would be daylit through the glazed risers and animated by the passing lift cars. Across the building, slower compartments, sharing shafts, move local traffic. Segmental service cores arranged behind the stiffened edges of the openings organize the floor layouts.

The premium on space set up by the tower's attenuation calls for the use of the highest-strength materials, concretes and steels, to minimize solid cross-sections. Science steadily improves tenacity without altering elasticity – the bond between molecules but not their resilience. Although the load environment is not extreme,

no earthquakes or outlandish winds, this extremely slender tower is very flexible.

In accordance with the project's ideals, the engineering response to this pliancy is theatrical. An active pendulum damper is installed within the crown of the building. Not only does the counterweight swing in response to movement, it is mechanically pushed by hydraulic actuators to react to accelerations detected by electronic sensors. Such a system is not original – others have been installed in Japanese skyscrapers to act in the extremity of a major earthquake – but this application represents the culmination of a personal odyssey for the structural designer. Nearly 30 years ago on the Centre Pompidou project in Paris, a change in engineers led to the formulation of the 'P-delta' effect. This name was given to the propensity of a very springy structure, once disturbed, to be dragged over by its own displaced weight. Cancelling this effect using a linear control mechanism is a new departure, notionally a very efficient use of resources. Active control keeps the very lightest frame at acceleration levels acceptable to the occupants. If a breakdown

occurs, movement escalates but passive action is still just sufficient to avoid overstressing. The principles needed to tune this system are well developed, an essential part of aeronautics and naval architecture, and there is a sparse elegance to this 'classical control theory' that is enjoyed by engineers. The equations describing motion can be recast into manageable form by switching 'domain' – the conceptual space in which the mathematician operates to make an otherwise intractable problem amenable to a solution procedure.

The application of feedback devices to very large buildings is heroic; the forces involved have grown very large. Avionic systems handle the 350 tonnes of a jumbo jet, ship stabilizers handle 40,000- or 50,000-tonne vessels. Depending on occupancy the tower could weigh more than 120,000 tonnes. Despite computerization, problems can still occur in the design of complicated systems: early prototypes of the space shuttle suffered control instability. Building applications will need very careful monitoring, assessment and adjustment when they eventually become commonplace.

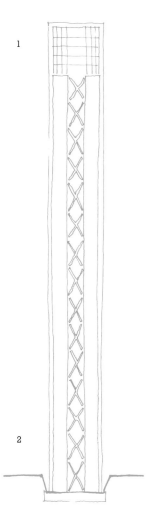

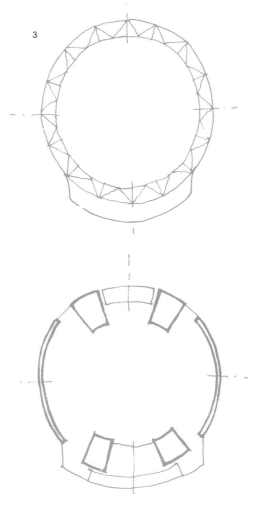

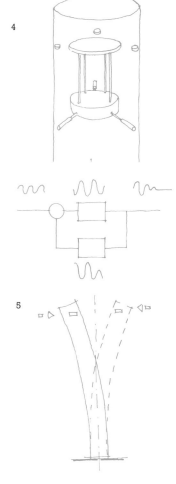

1. A stiff concrete hull at low level sets up a firm base for much lighter framing in the upper levels.

2. At ground level the tower disappears into an open well. The circular cofferdam surround is very efficient. This architectural device increasing the height of the tower is expensive.

3. Structure and vertical circulation are confined to the perimeter of the floor plates. By glazing the peripheral lift-cores, the hull openings necessary for access double up to bring light in.

4. Prone to wind excitation, the slender tube is protected by an active damping system. Actuators drive a counterweight in opposition to external forces.

5. In order to be effective mass dampers of 5–10 per cent of the structure weight may be required. Siting the dampers at the top of the tower compensates for the dominant mode of vibration.

Above: The armature is opened on two sides. The solid side-walls are then reconnected by multistorey braces. The damping system is featured within the glass crown.

Following page left: Structure on the outside is the most material-efficient arrangement for a narrow tower. Segmental spaces, and radial and curving floor beams add expanse.

Following page right: Within the pervasive strength of a single architectural idea the design is developed rigorously. Accommodation, structure and circulation are closely integrated.

61

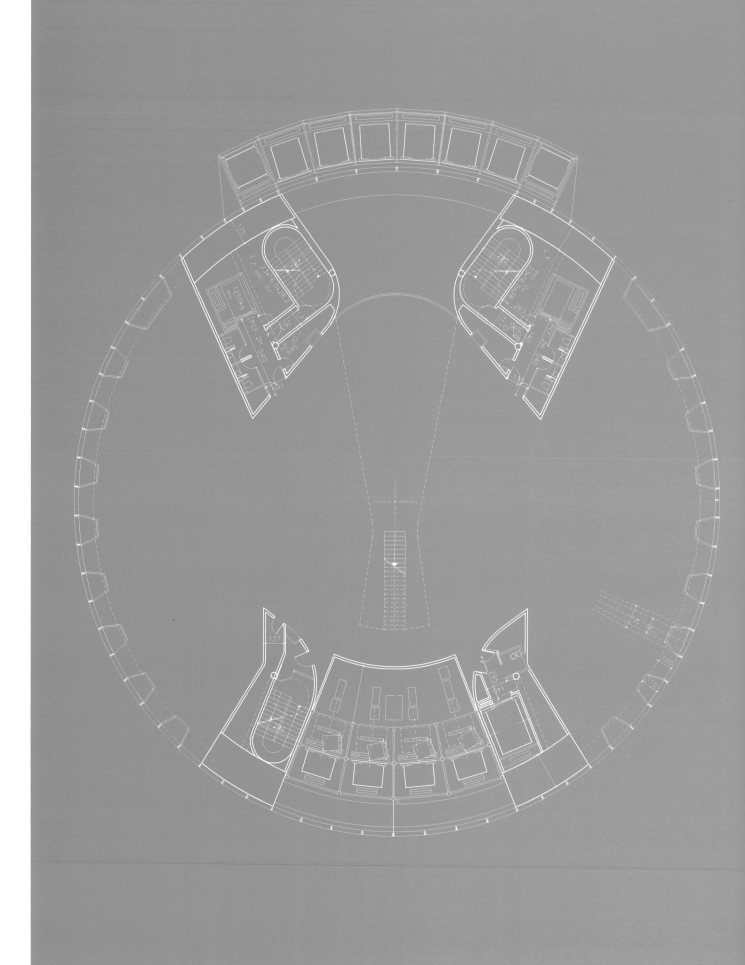

0   5m   10m   ⊘
         15ft 30ft

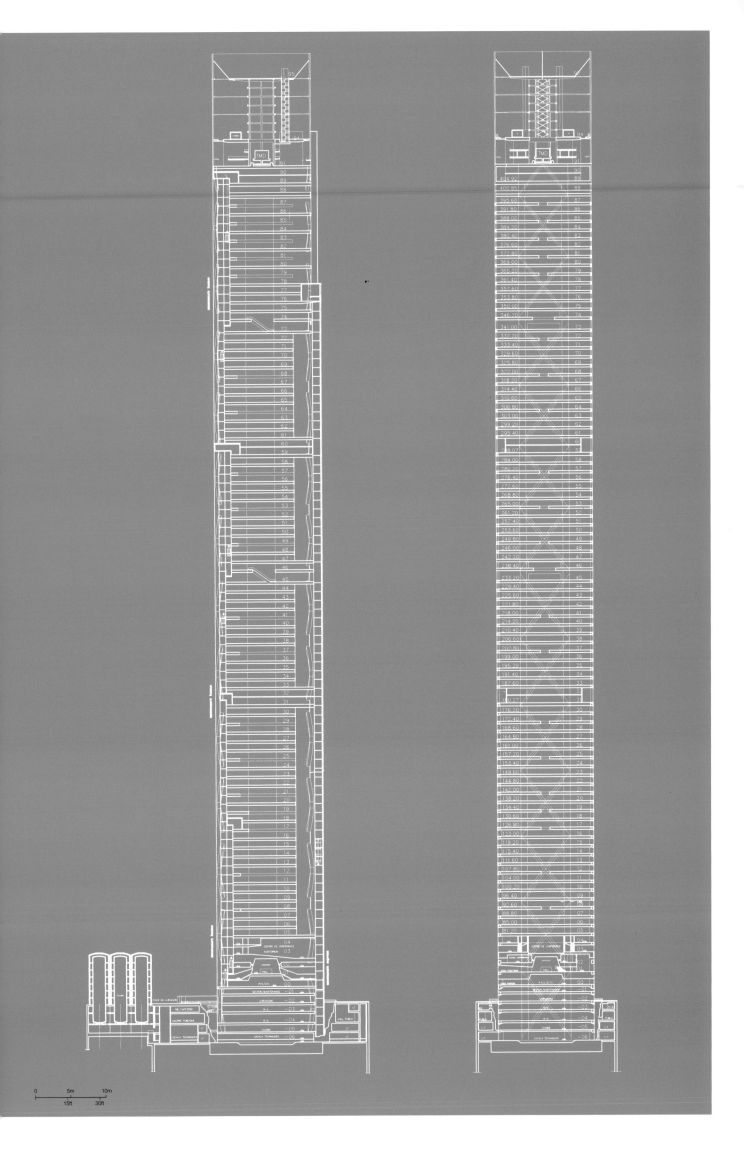

BUILDING TORRE AGBAR
LOCATION BARCELONA, SPAIN, 2004
ARCHITECT ATELIER JEAN NOUVEL
ENGINEER BRUFAU/OBIOL

This building is a unique departure using the most conventional of means. Out of 30 floors and four basements, levels one to 25 span between nested cylindrical concrete walls. The core is egg-shaped on plan, the perimeter elliptical, and the long axes of both shapes aligned roughly north by north-west to bisect the road system forking around the site – an orientation indifferent to prevailing winds and sun angles. Between the walls, floors are lightweight decks on steel beams pierced for service flexibility. Upper floors are prestressed reinforced concrete plates cantilevered off the central stem, all enclosed in a triangulated steel-framed dome of glass. The two components of the structure are sheathed in a continuous rainscreen of small glass panels, curving inwards to a recessed summit platform tha conceals cleaning gantries and aerial arrays. With immense sophistication the central core, lift shafts and overruns are capped off within the upper space.

The external form and surface treatment are a working through of a number of the architect's preoccupations. Jean Nouvel (born in 1945 in France) has systematically explored the sensory properties of large glass façades, veneered and layered with textures and finishes of varying reflectivity. In the western Mediterranean light, the reactive envelope of the Arab Institute in Paris with its mass of diaphragm shutters has become a Gaudí-esque mosaic of coloured glass panels, sprinkled with photovoltaic panels, and mounted on extruded, colour-anodized aluminium brise-soleil. Like the Catalan architect/saint's majolica-studded forms, the carefully contrived pattern of small panes, 120 centimetres by 30 centimetres (47 by 12 inches), will scatter light almost as small imperfections in fixing will scatter it. The slight resilience of the subframes in the wind will enhance the shimmer. Repeating the structural arrangement of the 1996 Tour Sans Fin project for Paris, the substance of the building evaporates with height. In the earlier project the ground-building interface problem was addressed by running the tower shaft on into a deep hole. In Torre Agbar this device is supplemented with a reflecting moat of water, going some way to correct the structure's squat proportioning.

The perimeter concrete wall is pierced by 4,400 different window openings, bringing variations in response to the expanding and contracting spaces of the otherwise conventional office floors. Deep, lined reveals reflect an even light within. The construction of the enclosing walls used a patented, climbing form system: mould panels were lifted a storey at a time, set up with pre-fabricated steel cages within, and then filled with concrete before being struck and lifted again. A central working platform rose ahead of the work, from which materials could be safely and effectively distributed. The complicated plan and section shapes

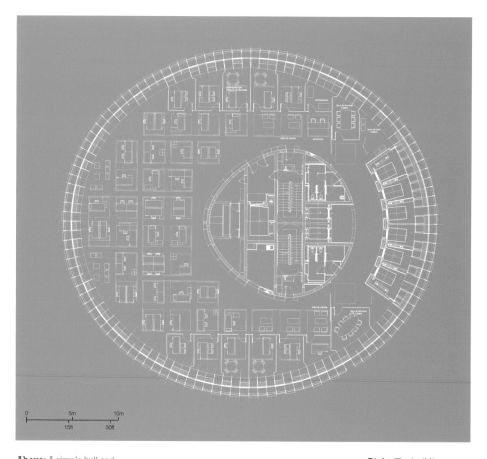

Above: A simple hull and core layout is given subtlety by adjusting a circular plan to acknowl-edge the asymmetries of European climate. An egg-shaped core generates different floor breadths.

Right: The building envelope uses layering, colour, pattern and reflectance to appropriate Antonio Gaudi's built form and response to Barcelona's light.

were reduced to economical components of circular radii.

The diaphanous effect sought in the façade treatment is strengthened by an anodized-aluminium cladding to the concrete walls, its lustrous reflectance backlighting the outer skin. The coloured-glass rainscreen, inner layers of glass and reflective metal all contribute to reducing solar gain. Electricity is generated on the building's surface and the massive concrete perimeter walls act as a heat sink, smoothing out thermal ebbs and flows through the building fabric. Up to floor 25 suspended ceilings and raised floors provide conventional distribution pathways for air-conditioning and IT. The open terraces above are provided with locally conditioned enclosures, meeting places and workspaces.

Floor plans are organized around the vertical circulation layout – in turn generated by the conical form of the building. A bank of lifts on the east wall serves the concrete-enclosed floors. A pair of lifts in the core passes on to the upper levels and a large service elevator sits under the highest point of the building. This disposition gives a clear orientation to the building, emphasizing the outlook to the north-west – away from the sea and towards the mountains inland. The envelope of the building is treated as a single wrap, leaving interior and environmental asymmetries unacknowledged.

The structure's stumpy tubes of reinforced concrete are ideally suited to resist any incoming seismic activity, which Barcelona's siting on the sand terraces between two river mouths tends to magnify. Four levels of basement containing parking act as a buoyant foundation to the superstructure. Each level of overburden (the mass of soil above the foundation level) removed compensates for six or seven storeys of space above. Stresses in the ground beneath the building are little altered by the new imposition, and substantial settlement is avoided.

The elements of the building are intended to be legible in the interior spaces. Within the upper-level enclosure the core becomes a single element, curving inwards onto shrinking ancillary accommodation to mirror the outer envelope. At ground level the entrance sequence comprises a bridge across a cleft showing the outer hull passing downwards, leading to a double-height entrance hall in which a cut-out with a descending staircase demonstrates the continuity of the inner core.

The simple concept of a building as an object brought into light is matched here by the well-mannered form, striking but unimposing, non-intrusive in the airstream and at ground level, practically and modestly husbanding its energy use. The ingenious use of established procurement to achieve a real conceptual change is exemplary.

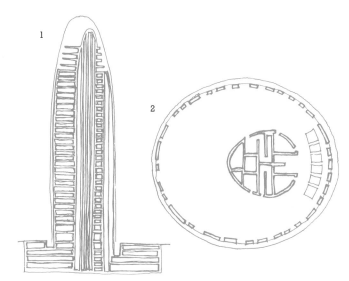
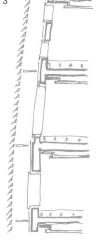

1. As the building rises its concrete hull gives way to ranks of floors, cantilevered from the central core and all enclosed in the continuous steel and glass envelope.

2. Devices explored elsewhere in the architect's work are explored and adapted to the circumstances of site and programme. The building is a southern European version of the Tour sans Fin.

3. The façade comprises an array of enamelled metal brise-soleil protecting a glass weathering of varying transparency.

4. The reinforced concrete hull and core structure is constructed using climbing form-work. Concrete is placed from a centrally located pump.

Opposite: The vertical circulation of the building is treated with great sophistication. The peripheral lifts stop off under the inward curve. The central core is topped off within the penthouse itself.

Above: A computer
rendering of the tower
with the Sagrada Familia
in the distance. The
shaped profile, rather
awkward on its cylindrical
shaft, is one response
to building tall in a
low-rise city.

BUILDING	HOTEL HABITAT, HOTEL HESPERIA & OFFICE TOWERS
LOCATION	BARCELONA, SPAIN, 2005
ARCHITECT	DOMINIQUE PERRAULT
ENGINEER	BRUFAU I ASSOCIATS/ PAMIAS INDUSTRIAL ENGINEERING

At a sufficient scale, building projects impinge directly on urban-design issues. The French architect Dominique Perrault uses architectural form directly in the resolution of town-planning issues. Appointed as design adviser to the mayor of Barcelona, he has used several local commissions to generate a consistent and conscientious approach to building high in an essentially horizontal city.

The project for the Hotel Habitat dismantles the form of the conventional tower block. A narrow shaft of bedroom accommodation occupies a zone identified by the architect as belonging to the 'vertical city', a conceptual space defined by Antonio Gaudí's Sagrada Familia cathedral and Barcelona's Olympic Village. This element is separated, by a horizontal dislocation, from a low-level block at the general height of the city's blocks, benchmarked by the Eixample (the 1859 extension of the old city with a low-rise grid plan).

The dislocation between front and back is given direction by the façade treatment. A glazed panel between hotel shaft and base rises vertically, implying a shearing movement upwards – as if the main

bedroom block had been lifted off its base. The cubic base, containing 'public interaction' spaces, is well grounded, the raised parallelepiped of withdrawing rooms, seemingly weightless. The architect identifies an innate humanity expressed in the fabric of the city of Barcelona. The anthropomorphic quality of this project is highlighted in a presentation comparison of the built form with an Easter Island statue.

The two other buildings completing the group, the Hotel Hesperia and associated Tower of Offices, take up these innovations. This hotel includes 114 rooms arranged on nine floors, forming a cube similar to the urban surroundings. The nearby office block, at 21 storeys, is topped by a four-storey overhang, which defines a large volume of space in front of the two buildings. Technically, these architectural devices require some structural gymnastics. The upper works of the buildings are all in reinforced concrete. The centre section of Hotel Habitat is cellular, and the plan layout of each floor elementary, so that there is an excess of cross-walls acting as cantilever fins reaching forward to pick up the 22 storeys of bedrooms. The overturning forces set up

Above: From left to right: Hotel Habitat, Hotel Hesperia and the Tower of Offices. Deep overhangs in the strong sunlight generate mobile shadows across the textured building surfaces.

by the building's form are transferred into these walls, which are kept from buckling sideways by the addition of the attached lift cores. The low-level 'tail' of public accommodation tends to balance out the overall weight of the building onto the site. Bending forces are carried down to ground level, and then into the car-parking basements, which extend under the entire site. The forces in the system are brought back under the superstructure in these levels, so that the foundations below are evenly loaded beneath the building's centre of gravity.

The enclosure of the Novates comprises pierced concrete walls, providing protection from heat gain and glare. Views are framed through a regular pattern of circular piercings, large anough to blur any distinctions between window-wall and brise-soleil. The single size of window used throughout gives the building surface a neutral grain, and leaves only one interface detail – the continuous window-jamb – to deal with in the entire envelope design. Internally, concrete pours are arranged during construction so that no 'daywork' joints are visible, all being hidden at floor or

Above: The punched window façades of the Hotel Habitat reduce glare within and emphasize the elementary volumes brought into the light.

internal-corner junctions. An outer layer of heavy plates of anodized aluminium – intended to reflect different qualities of light – provides a shield around the building, resistant to the maritime climate. This metal sheathing also masks external joints.

Variegated claddings break the shapes of the Hesperia and Tower of Offices. Glazed and opaque panels alternate in random patterns across the façades. Architectural renderings show the buildings dissolving into the sky.

The orthogonal grid of the city is carried through every part of these projects. The room volumes, plan layouts and structural elements are all set out with simple rectangular proportions. Exposed concrete soffits and walls contribute to the even tempering of internal spaces, and underscore the quality of stone finishes and fine metal detailing. The underlying form of the city is present in the structure and organization of the building, but there is no other history. The rooms are rationally arranged cells, with fittings planted directly onto the elemental structure. This simplicity is not straightforward in terms of construction. Services, conduits, lights and switch boxes must be carefully coordinated into the structural drawings, and fixed at the same time as the reinforcement but to a much higher level of accuracy. Errors can only be corrected by disfiguring the self-finishing surfaces, or by condemning large sections of work.

Architectural-quality concrete finishes are always difficult to attain: as well as avoiding surface defects, achieving an even coloration requires considerable skill. 'Congestion', due to the addition of embedded service runs, aggravates the problems. The standard room patterns mean that high-tolerance steel form-work, with hinged and well-sealed components, can be specially designed, prefabricated and reused throughout the job to achieve consistent, best-quality facings to the exposed concrete.

Above: The deep soffits of the two tall buildings are aligned with surrounding cornices to imply and reinforce the volume of the public space.

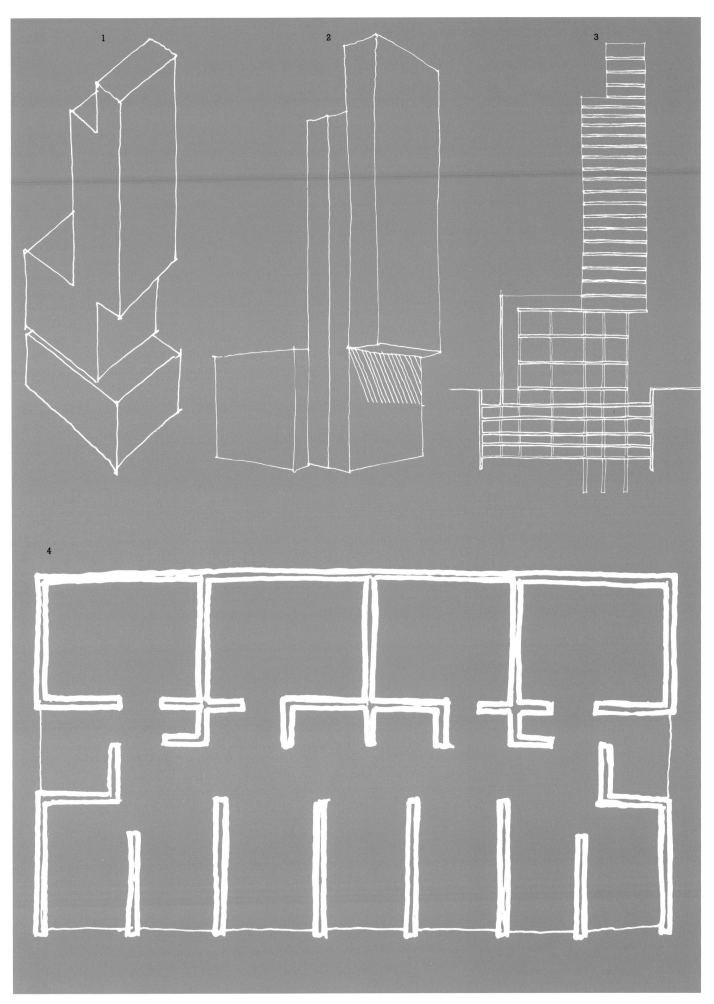

1. The deep basements of the Hotel Habitat extend forward under the entire building to take advantage of ground displacement. The excavation balances the new structure's weight.

2. By setting the over-hangs high, the relatively steep sun-angles of the southern city generate big shadows on the façades without darkening the public square.

3. The overhanging accommodation gener-ates extra loads immediately behind the lower façade – like the fulcrum of a see-saw. Columns and foundations are enlarged locally.

4. The simple rectangular plans generate stiff concrete cross-walls. These elements reach forward to carry the cantilevered spaces without the need for an expensive transfer plate.

Above: The highly
articulated bulk of the
tower – medium-rise
blocks of offices
suspended between
structural 'quoins' –
allows it a place in the
lower-level surroundings
of central Frankfurt.

The reconciliation of tall buildings with human ecology remains very much a work in progress amongst contemporary architects and environmental engineers. In Germany, the European country with the strongest Green Party lobby, a major institution has set out to provide a prototype for an ecological tower. The Commerzbank headquarters in Frankfurt am Main, Germany's financial centre, is a contribution to the design debate.

A competition outcome, the scheme seeks a radical reinterpretation of high-rise living and working. Characteristically, Foster and Partners reduced the complicated brief requirements to a set of axiomatic ideals. A summary sketch shows a seat by an openable window, from which colleagues and a garden can be seen nearby with the city skyline beyond.

In order to achieve natural ventilation in a north European climate the built form is completely reconceived, turning away from a conventional core and surrounding floor arrangement. The precedents of Oscar Niemeyer's Tête Défense scheme of 1967 with 'sky gardens' dividing up blocks of vertical accommodation, and Roche & Dinkeloo's Knights of Columbus Building with wide-span floors bearing onto quoins of circulation cores, are combined on a triangular plan around a central atrium. Eight storeys of accommodation (a division determined by potential leasing arrangements) alternate with four of gardens in a helical pattern so that internal windows are always overlooking a garden and, beyond that, the city.

Glass screens enclosing these 'winter gardens' and set across the atrium space control internal air movements set up by winds and the buoyancy of warm air. Automatic vents adjusting to and compensating for the manually operated opening lights keep the pressure differentials low to preclude draughts and door-opening problems. Transparent bulkheads also serve in the fire strategy of the building, providing

Above: Views across the open core, and the provision of double-height spaces in addition to the principal sky gardens, contribute to a feeling of spaciousness throughout the building.

smoke reservoirs into which hot gases can be corralled and prevented from cooling and dispersing dangerously throughout the building. Computational fluid dynamics, or CFD, a crossover from aerodynamics, has been an essential tool in releasing these manipulations of airflows on plan and section. Although calibration with supplementary wind-tunnel testing is essential, the programmes allow flows of gas and energy to be rapidly predicted, adjusted and reassessed within a fluent design process.

Large-scale air-conditioning, sealing the building and blowing tempered and humidity-controlled air through it, becomes unbalanced when occupants are allowed to open windows at whim. Instead a so-called 'mixed mode' servicing strategy must be adopted. For a large part of the year in temperate latitudes and within a continental land mass outside air, if it is clean enough, can be used to make surroundings comfortable. Then, only the partial

provision of services – radiant heating and cooling; forced ventilation; air heating, cooling and humidity control – will be required for the remainder of the time and can be run by an automated building-management system. The initial costs of a full provision of plant, and the potential inefficiencies of running it below capacity for extended periods, are avoided at the expense of a few days each year when exceptional circumstances may overwhelm the reduced plant provisions.

At construction, the tower was the tallest in Europe, overtopping a neighbour by some 2 metres (7 feet). Vertical circulation, accommodation and structure are all clearly defined but integrated into a simple composition – the nine hanging gardens giving a balanced tripartite division of each elevation which steps up to the secular spire of a telecom array. The dispersal of floor plates makes for a broader silhouette, efficient for structure and land use at the expense of higher envelope costs. Placing

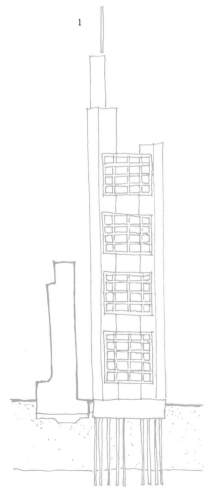

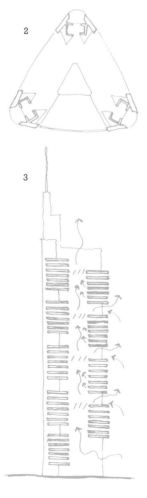

1. The main office floors span onto multi-storey 'Virendeel' girders in each façade. These are in turn supported on the building's corners.

2. Cores concentrated in corners are ideally located to provide efficient lateral resistance. The triangular plan makes for expensive floor framing.

3. Cross-sections are arranged to develop natural ventilation patterns. Airflows within the central atrium are controlled by a series of horizontal diaphragms framed with space-decks.

4. The building rests on deep concrete piles, bored in diminishing diameters like inverted telescopes and pre-stressed to reduce elastic shortening. The piled foundation runs deep in

order to minimize soil deformation. The draw-down of adjacent structures is inevitable but more dispersed because the deeper loads are delivered into the soil mass.

Above: The full-width girder frames on each façade allow the sky gardens to be uninterrupted spaces of sufficient height to allow daylight into the centre of the building.

occupants next to less-costly internal walls mitigates the expense of the extensive surfaces.

The extremism of the design leads to several incongruities, and the competition entry was controversial even within the originator's office. The triangular plan extends the perspectives of the internal views. It pervades the corner cores – containing lifts, stairs and risers – on the outside, and conference spaces opening directly off the circulation concentrations in the enclosed inner corners. The glass menisci across the atrium are carried on tetrahedral space-frames. The geometry breaks down in the main floors, which revert to orthogonal layouts – a dissonance recovered by the beautiful outwards bow imparted to each outer wall.

The logic of the building does not acknowledge the asymmetry of the sun's path. It is effectively two wings of accommodation embracing a void and garden, and the rotation of the plan may develop a complexity of space at the expense of not making the best use of natural light.

The reinforced-concrete cores were rapidly erected on sliding formwork with climbing cranes. The accommodation blocks are steel-framed, lightweight composite floors of concrete and steel sheeting spanning onto multi-storey welded frames on the outer faces of the building. Cut sheeting and complicated intersections to meet the irregular plan shape make the decks uneconomic. The outer 'Vierendeel' frames – girders comprising columns and spandrel beams, bending together as a unit – are inherently inefficient. Stabilized sideways by the stiffness of the adjacent floors, they readily assimilate the plan's curvatures. Despite the complexities of joints and junctions a rigorous rationalization of interfaces allowed the contractor to achieve the three-days-per-floor construction rate essential for economy.

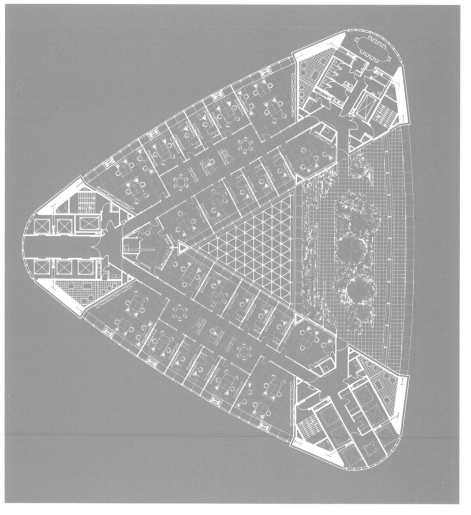

Top: The worker on the inside of the building is provided with a view back through its centre to his or her neighbour and out to the city across the adjacent sky garden.

Above: The hierarchy of the structure allows large spaces to be dispersed through the building and natural light to penetrate throughout the deep plan.

Above: The plan is squared up within the three sides using residual and open-plan spaces to change the grid. This simplifies the structure, partitioning, floor and ceiling linings.

Above: The spiralling
levels of the building
allow it to be terminated
in a rising sweep towards
a telecom finial.
Movement through the
corner cores enlivens the
building's aspect.

BUILDING	DEBIS HOUSE, POTSDAMER PLATZ
LOCATION	BERLIN, GERMANY, 1999
ARCHITECT	RENZO PIANO BUILDING WORKSHOP/CHRISTOPH KOHLBECKER
ENGINEER	BOLL AND PARTNER

Won in competition in 1992 this scheme is a paradigm of north European high-rise design. It occupies a city block within the old urban structure of Berlin's Potzsdamer Platz and represents a reappraisal of the place and its nineteenth-century traditions. The first modern urban transport hub, the area was destroyed in the Second World War and subsequently bisected by the Berlin Wall. Today it has become part of the 'Daimler City' redevelopment, a comprehensive master plan. The building form is subdivided to echo the grain of the surrounding city. A 22-storey tower on the western end addresses the scale of the urban road network at the entrance to the Tiergarten tunnel. An ancient building technology is embedded in the completely modern, rationalized building envelope. Each elevation reflects its orientation and

comprises a carefully balanced composition of elements, assembled with an eye to proportion and repose, in its simple structuring. The ground plan incorporates an arcade of public space, linking site access points to the four blocks above.

Layout, fabric and details appear to have been worked out from first principles. The natural conditioning of accommodation and office spaces is a principal concern. The long site is arranged around a large central atrium giving floor plates of width suitable to daylighting and natural ventilation. There is a close reading here of Louis Kahn's A.N. Richards Medical Laboratories: the separation of vertical circulation, stairs and lifts from the main accommodation produces an efficient plan, which can be fitted to an irregular site and generate a picturesque composition of parts. This

Above: The south end of the mixed development is composed of vertical circulation and service elements framing accommodation blocks behind solar-control screens.

80

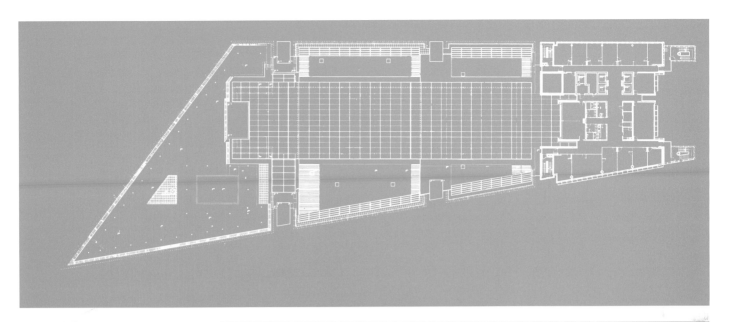

Top: The plan fills an entire city block, organizing the site into regular articulated components dimensioned to suit daylight and circulation provisions.

Above: The north corner is handled effortlessly. Floor slabs cantilever off a single column to support cladding that gradually condenses onto an almost sheared arris.

hierarchy of organization is underscored by the main structure. Two levels of basement car-park descend tentatively into the saturated glacial gravels beneath Berlin and support a two-storey 'table' of transfer structure, which straddles the perimeter arcade and mezzanine cock-lofts. The structure above is a conventional frame, core-braced. Service staircases are appended to the corners, cantilevering as scissor stairs over the public spaces below. The roof of the atrium is a lightweight canopy carried on space framing and the blocks are edged by quoin-like vertical shafts. The highest service tower is crowned in an incongruous cube of copper-clad panelling.

West and south elevations are 'breathing' façades. Two glazed layers act as a solar chimney in summer, channelling hot air up and away, and as a greenhouse in winter, buffering the interior and extending the thermal gradient through the wall. An outer layer of louvres is sensor controlled, opening wide on hot summer nights. The double-glazed inner panes are hopper opening, and natural ventilation is practical for about 60 per cent of the year when the outside temperature is above 5°C (410°F) and below 20°C (680°F). On the other sides of the buildings a double-glazed skin is protected by extruded-terracotta screens, a natural khaki- coloured fired earth lending great subtlety and depth to the surfaces. An intermediate layer of adjustable blinds finished in a matching colour completes the build-up of the façades. The balance of solid to void in these walls means that the blinds can be operated more or less randomly without detracting from the composition. The materials palette coincides with the changing colours of the surrounding trees and daylight conditions reflecting across the moving panes. The standard elements of the brise-soleil system are carefully spaced on the basis of lighting studies to allow the best compromise of daylight, and glare and heat reduction to the interior. The supporting frames for terracotta and glass are understated, with delicate detailsof struts and hinges. Opening lights of fritted, frameless, toughened glass, supported on glued patch hinges, record a technology transfer from the car industry whose heirs still occupy the site. The crispness of the low technology sits well with the sophisticated simplicity of the support systems.

The envelope treatment is wrapped around into the atrium of the building.

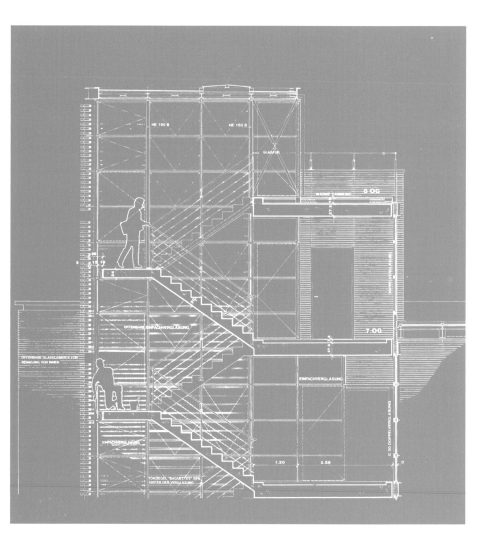

Above: The perimeter stairwells of the building are secondary lightweight structures. Attached to the main frame the flights are enclosed in finely detailed glass shafts with external sunshades.

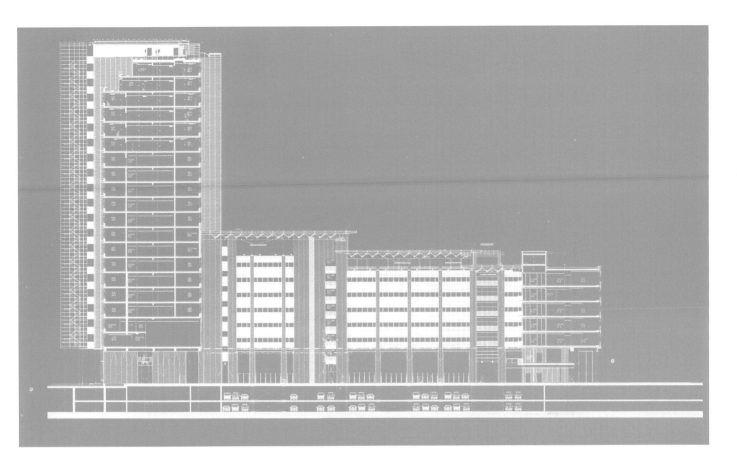

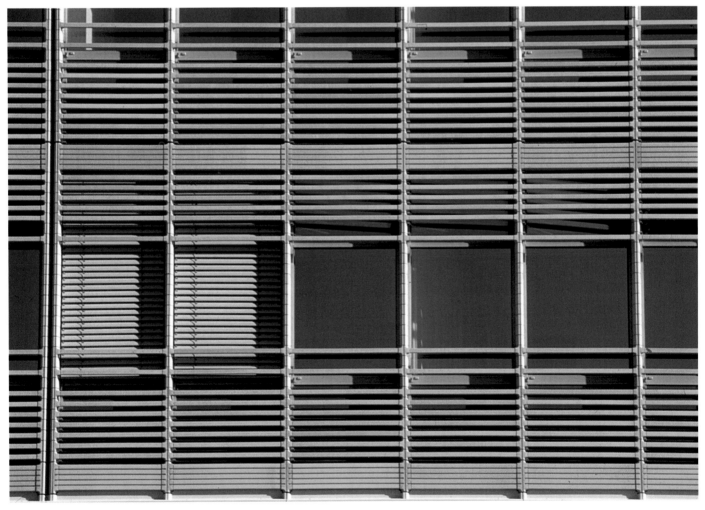

Top: The building is organized around a longitudinal atrium toplit and roofed with a glazed space-frame. Two levels of car-parking basement fill the site.

Above: The terracotta brise-soleil comprises crosspieces of extruded ceramic supported on spigot ends concealed behind moulded pottery mullions.

Debis House

The glass roof is louvred, opening to disperse build-ups of hot air which otherwise would radiate uncomfortably downwards, and to promote cross-ventilation across the accommodation blocks. Direct sunlight is modulated by silk-screen patterns on the glass surfaces, and acoustic treatments are added to reduce noise from the public ground level disturbing the surrounding offices.

Mechanical systems activate under extremes of internal load or outside environment. They are made as efficient as possible. Heat and power comes from a district heating system. Cooling is delivered by water-chilled ceiling panels, a strategy avoiding the ventilation losses of tempered air while keeping the building structure in even conditions. Rain water is recycled in the building, irrigating all the planting and flushing the toilets. So-called non-deleterious materials were used throughout the scheme; even concrete moulds had to be prepared for casting with plant oil. Local pollution was minimized by handling and pre-assembling materials in the redundant railway yards nearby, and waste removal was kept off the roads by shipping it out along the adjoining Landwehr Canal.

The scheme has been particularly influential in Europe, widening perceptions of the possibilities inherent in building-envelope design.

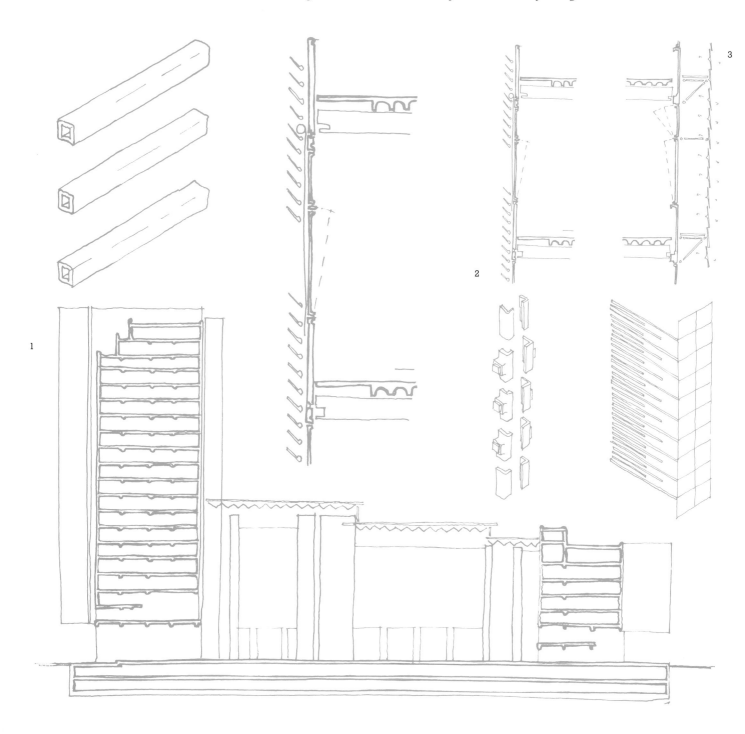

1. The frames of the low-rise blocks can bend to resist wind loads with no additional lateral bracing. The tall tower is stiffened by lift shaft and core walls.

2. The low-maintenance brise-soleil are constructed in the simplest of assemblies. The natural earth colour reduces glare and weathers perfectly.

3. A double-skin façade buffers the interior by allowing air to circulate within an intermediate space containing adjustable blinds to carry heat away.

Right: Light is diffused throughout the atrium. As much as possible is collected by the fully glazed roof, then modulated by soffit screens and reflected all around by white glass baffles along the walls.

BUILDING **DEUTSCHE POST**
LOCATION **BONN, GERMANY, 1999**
ARCHITECT **MURPHY/JAHN**
ENGINEER **WERNER SOBEK**

The new headquarters of the Deutsche Post in the old government quarter of Bonn is the outcome of an open design competition. In pursuing a progressive corporate policy in the 'greenest' of European countries, the client's principal requirement for a design to embrace low-energy-use concepts became mixed with a desire to express accountability and accessibility to the public and to promote communication and interaction amongst its employees. During construction the organization changed from being called Deutsche Post to become instead World Net. The name change is a reminder of the need to match the protean role of a national mail service, responding to the changes in global communications, with truly flexible accommodation. Specific objectives included setting the build cost at minimum market levels only, but seeking energy savings 25 per cent below European energy norms. In outcome, the designers claim a 40 per cent reduction in typical operating costs for the same initial build cost as a comparable conventional building.

The winning scheme by Murphy/Jahn has the characteristic hallmarks of experienced designers. The standard office block – a by-product of the German economic miracle – has been taken and transformed by knowledge gained working simultaneously in Chicago and West Germany for several decades. The design is understated, mixing simplicity in layout with sophistication in detail, and carefully refined in all its elements. Sited between the town and the park areas of the Rhine meadows adjacent to the river, the project completes a larger composition of buildings incorporating Behnisch's old parliament building (now a conference centre), Egon Eiermann's 'Langer Eugen' Tower (now occupied by the UN) and the broadcasting station Deutsche Welle by Joachim Schürmann & Partner.

The layout is a sophisticated alternative to the usual tower poised over a plinth. The vertical element is allowed to develop fully, with the horizontal plinth sweeping up but separated from the column. This arrangement makes the complicated structural transfers usually necessary at podium level irrelevant, and makes the building formally and practically easy to read. Meeting the ground without inflection, the tower appears accessible and relaxed. The plinth structures and approach ramps complete the upper terrace of the riverside park. As well as office accommodation, both elements enclose a variety of conference halls, bars, restaurants, book stores and multi-purpose halls.

The tower itself is a variant of a well-tested form. Two elliptical segments are split and sheared about a central, circulation and orientation space. The frame is reinforced concrete: simple flat slabs supported on circular columns and core walls. A close column grid, suited to the mainly cellular office provision, keeps the structural depth of each floor to a minimum, reducing the overall height and weight of the building. The circulation pattern is simple and uncomplicated, with lift banks opening into the longitudinal foyers. The curve of the corridors between outer offices and central conference spaces avoids an institutional reference. The stair and lift shafts on either side of the central divide brace the main frames and are coupled with steel outriggers at every ninth floor of the 45 in total. These links coincide with sky gardens: platforms dividing the building into vertical compartments and on which cross-circulation and local orientation can take place. The close integration of structure and overall organization is carried through to the environmental-control provisions. The built form and its details take account of a series of practical and ecologically sound natural conditioning devices.

Human comfort depends on an environment combining well-tempered air and surroundings with balanced and mild surface temperatures. Air heats and cools the skin by conduction, remote surfaces radiate if hot or draw energy if cold.

Concrete is a good heat store. In the office spaces soffits are unlined, the exposure of as-struck reinforced concrete being made economic by recent improvements in standard formwork quality. The mass of the building acts as a thermal flywheel, the even temperature of the concrete overhead contributing to the office ambience. Heating is provided by cast-iron water piping, cast within the concrete so that the whole slab becomes a radiator to the surrounding spaces. Cool air can be channelled across the slabs at night to remove excess summer heat.

The other principal radiant surface in the building, the external walls, comprise a double-skin glass system. Allowing maximum daylight provision, and reducing the energy drain of artificial light at the expense of inferior insulation and the problem of controlling excessive solar heating, the fully glazed envelope of the tower delivers the requisite transparency and openness. Glass is everywhere in the building. Once the decision was taken to make a fully glazed building, the project could be interpreted largely as an exercise in glass technology. The cellular offices are divided by glass screens, with noise-reducing glazed units and sliding doors to open out the boxes. Sky gardens have structural glass floors, and the fire escapes have linings of fire-resistant glass. Altogether 47 different types of glass unit are incorporated in the building – all white glass, free of iron impurities which give the characteristic green tinge. This expensive specification

Above: Standing on the gently sloping bank of the Rhine, the simple tower form is separated from adjacent accommodation. All the façades are transparent and elegantly detailed.

gives the building an extraordinary sparkle and lightness of feel. The transparency of the glass is 91 per cent compared with 85 per cent for ordinary windows.

The inner skin of the outer walls acts as the seal on the building; it is a standard double-glazing curtain-wall system, argon-filled to improve insulation. On the other side of an accessible space containing blinds protected from the weather is an outer single layer of glass, configured differently on north and south sides but all supported on an attenuated system of brackets, hangers and 'wind needles' – lightweight spokes holding the surface out against the wind. The inside face of this outer sheet is sprayed with a low-emissivity coating to reflect radiant energy back into the building and reduce heat loss.

To the south the outer panes of glass are arranged as sloping shingles. In probably the most subtle part of a sophisticated project the panels are sized to be just adequate as a laminate of two 8 millimetre (5/16 inch) layers,

the cheapest practical glass covering. Within the overlaps, well-weathered opening panels are arranged, linked by cable actuators. In sunlight the thermal gradient across the wall is hot between outer layer and blind, cooler between blind and inner leaf. Open ventilators allow a stack effect to draw heat off at high level. A disadvantage of double-skin wall systems is the need to keep this sort of outer hot area under control, stopping the air dispersing inwards or developing huge updraughts.

In cooler weather air is allowed in through the outer skin and then into the building at the slab edge, is warmed in the intermediary zone, and finally passes across radiant heaters if necessary before being introduced into the office spaces. Airflows then continue into the central spaces of the building, to vent at the top of each atrium level. The vertical division of the building prevents excessive stack flows developing, which would cause draughts and pressures making doors difficult to operate.

Above: The walls of the tower slide out beyond the corners and above the cornice. The screens are lightly framed without an outside edge.

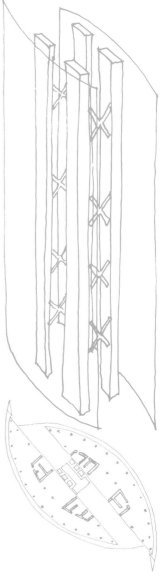

Above: Effectively comprising two adjacent buildings the tower is linked across a central atrium by a series of cross-braces and communal deck spaces.

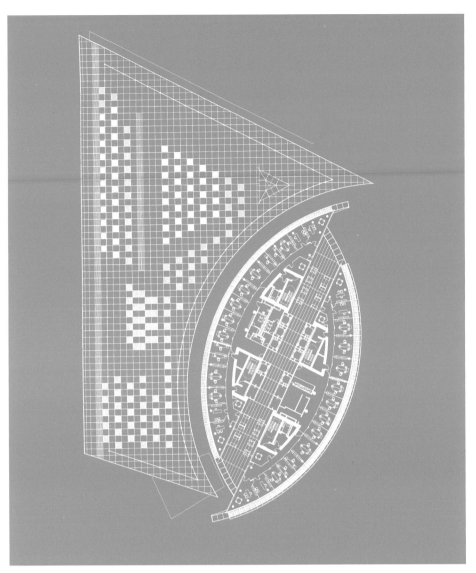

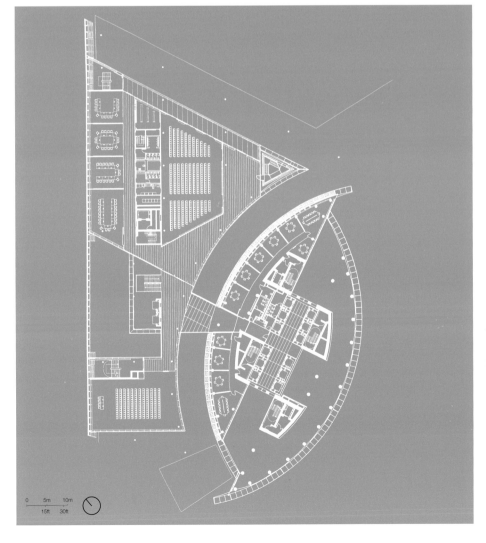

0   5m   10m
15ft   30ft

Top left: The tower floors are generally divided into cellular offices. Lift cores run within the central divide which is floored in at every ninth level.

Top: At roof level the façade rises as a screen, protecting penthouses and terraces without compromising the surrounding prospect. The building profile appears uncluttered.

Left: Ancillary accommodation and an auditorium are housed in an adjacent block leaving the main tower to be a simple structure without transfer elements or other structural complexity.

Above: A double-skin envelope, different on each elevation, minimizes the building's energy use. An external skin, sized to be of the thinnest glass, is held out on 'wind needles'.

The complexity and space requirement of the outer skin are justified in cost terms by the reduction in plant and plant space due to the absence of centralized air-handling. Duct work, particularly risers, is also profligate in space if noisy high-pressure flows are to be avoided. The net lettable office space gained is claimed to outweigh the loss of perimeter area.

Airflows in and around the building were extensively studied using computational fluid dynamics backed by wind-tunnel testing. Airflows across the building's face were matched with the behaviour within the envelope, which in turn was coupled to movements in the larger internal spaces. The behaviour of fire was also studied at the same time. By injecting a traceable oil dispersion into the simulated fume models it was possible to show the dilution levels of smoke moving away from a fire, and prove that escape routes would retain adequate visibility and breathability in the worst of situations.

The results of wind and thermal models were used to programme the building-management system, the automatic control of permeability and mechanical plant. Centralized computerized systems reacting to local sensor provisions are essential if the overall energy use of the building is to remain balanced. The principal losses in most modern buildings do not stem from poor construction or plant provisions, but simply from inefficient and uncontrolled operation.

The form of the building works well in the airstream. The main façades are extended beyond the footprint of the tower – an architectural device etherealizing the silhouette, which was also found to reduce wind noise in the corner offices. Similarly the top of the building eschews a cornice in favour of a vanishing continuation upwards which also provides an 11-metre (36-foot)-high screen to the penthouses and rooftop terraces.

Above: The central divide of the building, open entrance hall and elementary structure produce a highly legible building.

Above: The gently curving plan, economic in concrete flat-slab framing, improves corridor spaces. Internal partitions are glazed wherever possible.

BUILDING **COLORIUM**
LOCATION **DÜSSELDORF,**
GERMANY, 2001
ARCHITECT **ALSOP ARCHITECTS**
ENGINEER **ARUP GMBH**

Regeneration areas in the industrial cities of northern Europe tend to bring forth a particular kind of architecture. A relaxation of restrictions, a belief that spectacular design will stimulate development, a cheapness and transitoriness of construction, and a general brashness mark those areas specially designated for rescue from post-industrial blight. Into these zones, whose vestigial auras often remain, come experimental architects and their adventurous patrons.

The Colorium, a speculative office development in the Düsseldorf docklands beside the Rhine, takes its place in the rejuvenation of a dilapidated city quarter and its transformation into the *Mediahafen*, concentrating a new generation of electronics entrepreneurs in Germany's city of communication. Alongside a zoo of 'signature' buildings by celebrated architects on the Speditionsstrasse peninsula, the building replaces, in size and siting, an old silo.

The plan layout and structure are conventional. A concrete frame with circular perimeter columns is braced by an offset core positioned along the south side. Standard flexible partitions divide the floors into a range of lettable spaces. Architectural and technical sophistication are concentrated into the veneer of cladding. The orthodox curtain-walling system achieves a unique effect through an intense concentration on its decorative potential. Glass panels, windows and spandrels are mounted in prefabricated aluminium frames. 17 panel types are silk-screen printed with 30 colours in a pattern devised to break the scale and shape of the basic tower block. The architect is a fine artist in his own right and, like the English Vorticists co-opted into camouflaging ships against sea and sky with dazzle-painting during the First World War, he uses pattern, blurring the legibility of the storey heights and overscaling the relatively small 18-storey structure. Colours are restricted in the window fields, and the silk-screen matrix

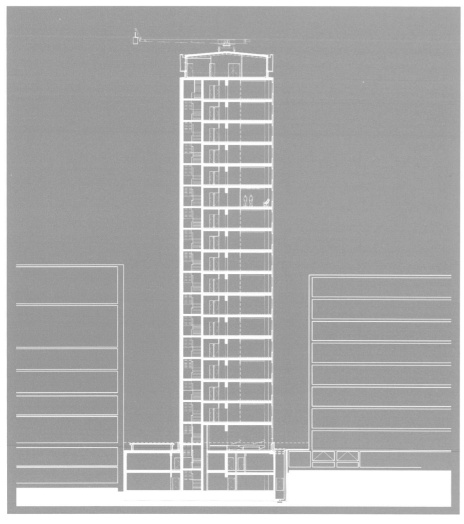

Above: A speculative office block in reinforced concrete framing, with downstand beams and simple curtain walling, is inserted between warehouses alongside a redundant wharf.

Far right: The banality of the structure is obliterated under a technicolour cloak. A standard configuration of ribbon window and spandrel panel becomes the ground for skin-deep decoration.

made less opaque – encouraging a perceptual depth, reinforced by reflections. Ambiguity is maintained by emphasizing the core structure with a different composition of panels.

The building terminates in a red light-box that conceals plant and cantilevers forward on steel truss-frames over the wharf frontage. This element completes the local and long-distance engagement of the building with its surroundings, reflecting in the water and, at night, visible across the city.

The achievement here is in the pragmatic exploitation of established technologies. The processing know-how of the signage industry, its abilities to generate and apply superficial complexity, have been combined with modern construction's façade expertise. Since the Second World War, the German and Swiss 'Mittlestand' manufacturing base has perfected curtain-walling systems. Aluminium, high up in the table of elements, is readily reactive and therefore resistant to corrosion. Extruded through dies, it can be cheaply formed into sections with complicated profiles ideally suited to frames of just the right adequacy for transportation and site assembly. Profiles can incorporate seals, which make mounting joints immediately weatherproof while tolerating movement in the underlying structure. In this instance, storey-height panels are placed, at a rate of 1½ storeys a day, to achieve an early weathertight date – essential to economic construction. Horizontal joints are arranged under the window sills, away from the floor-level mounting brackets, dispersing complexity. The building is naturally ventilated and every other window-pane is arranged to open, a reliable top-hung sash, simplifying the mullion joints and seals.

The double-glazed infills, with low-emissivity coatings, are decorated using 'serigraphic' printing. This mechanized process, using viscous ink forced through nylon, grew out of the poster stencils that become 'high art' in the hands of the 1920s Dutch De Stijl masters. The resulting fast runs, with very high colour quality and definition, now find a new application in the appropriation of that group's architectural motif of bright colour planes.

Representing the new 'media harbour', the planes and blocks of colour make a hammy reference to data files, like 1960s film credits denoting computer processing. The pattern looks like nothing so much as the BBC test card, the first electronically generated image, which occupied a transitional stage as it reflected George Hersee's famous hand-collaged composition – card F – of 1967. The elevation drawings of the building are included in journal presentations as abstract colour matrices. The building's façade treatment plugs back into the media: the way photographs, cropped and their perspective corrected, adorn magazine and book covers.

This is a plain building, clothed in a fabric that may be as ephemeral as its styling. Dye chemistry develops, but certain colours remain fugitive and the weathering of this wide palette will be instructive. The Colorium is a decorated box, precisely answering the questions posed by its brief. The clever way that technology has been manipulated to make something unique on a strict budget will expand into something more as manufacturing techniques permeate the industry and cross-fertilize. Computer-generated complexity can economically replace standardization, not just on the surface but throughout the physical process of building and on into its conceptual background.

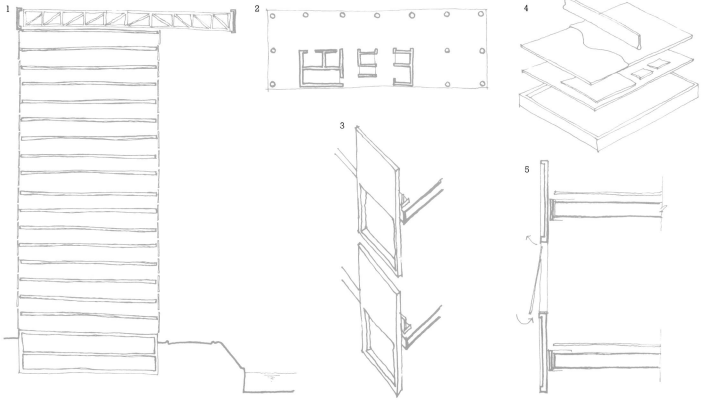

Left: Both window glass and opaque apron are overprinted with colour blocks. A sign-making process becomes the expression utilized in the project.

1. The cornice of the building is steel-framed and surrounded by a coloured-glass light-box. Basements take the structure down below the wharf to firm ground.

2. The simplest in-situ reinforced-concrete frame braced by an offset core is adopted for the structure. The circular columns do not interfere with the simplicity of the external envelope.

3. The cladding comprises floor-mounted panellized units. Placing horizontal joints above the window heads brings the sealing detail away from the main fixings.

4. An automated silk-screen printing process produces the variegated panels cheaply, precisely and with vivid colourings.

5. Natural ventilation is provided for with sill and high-level transom vents. Manually operated, the flaps provide reliable, adjustable and sealable openings.

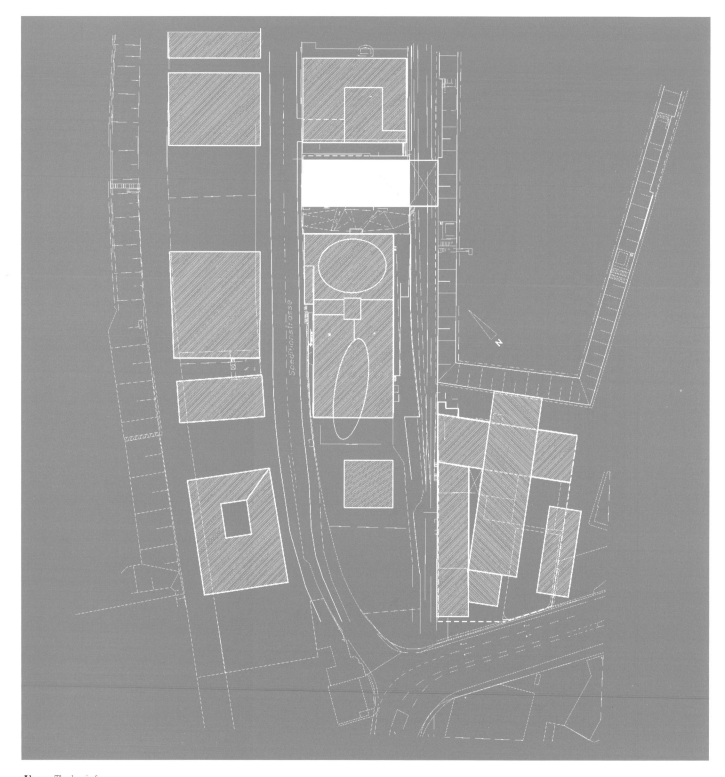

Above: The basic form
of the building, its scale,
plan and cornice over-
hanging the wharfside,
fits seamlessly into the
surroundings of the city's
docklands.

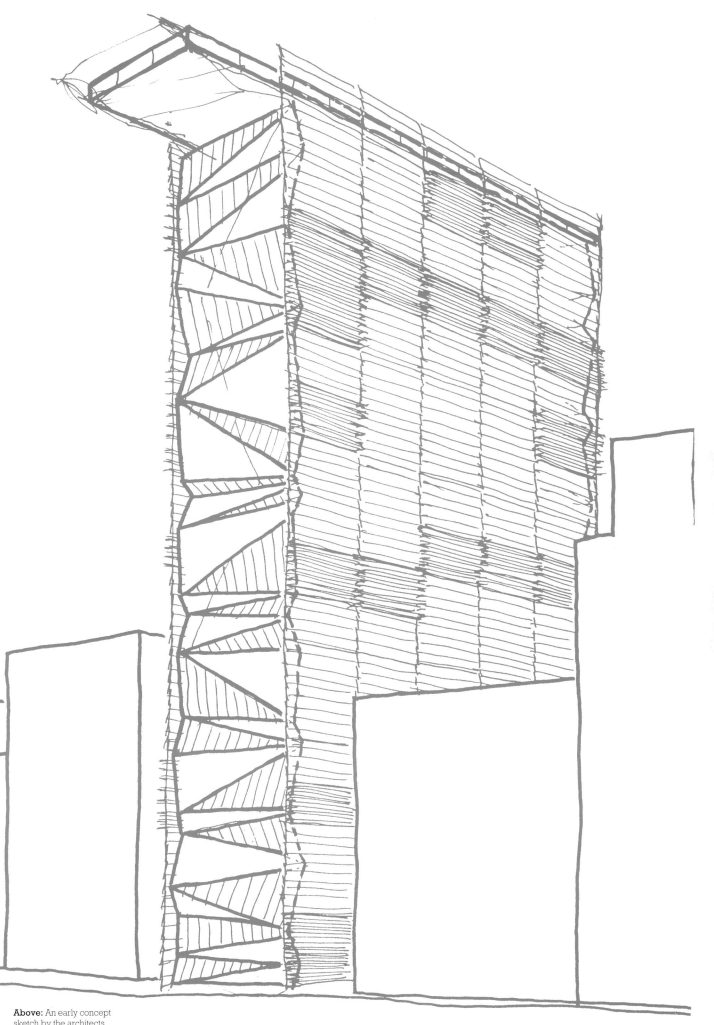

Above: An early concept
sketch by the architects
showing how a strong
idea can remain valid
after even the most
drastic simplification.

BUILDING   UPTOWN MÜNCHEN
LOCATION   MUNICH, GERMANY, 2003
ARCHITECT   INGENHOVEN OVERDIEK
            ARCHITEKTEN
ENGINEER   BURGGRAF, WEICHINGER
            AND PARTNER

In the 1980s a preoccupation of office-building designers was the maximization of usable space within the building envelope. Ingenuity went into getting the most lettable space out of the enclosing shell. Columns were squeezed into wall lines or moved outside, façade panels incorporated water heating within their thickness to reclaim radiator space. This drive for economy, particularly in the speculative development sector, sits uneasily with the evolution of double-skin wall systems. Their modulated daylighting effects and potential for natural conditioning are bought at the expense of space and complexity; barrier, frame and fixings are all doubled. And so investigations into, and improvements of, single-skin systems continue. The building envelope is considered as a single layer into which thermal modification, light control and permeability are all compressed.

The speculative Uptown München development occupies a city block in the Bavarian capital near the Olympic Stadium. Conceived as a self-contained town within the city, the complex is carefully sited to integrate with public transport systems.

Access planning is fundamental to a sustainable urbanism: the tower's basement incorporates an underground train station that links with the city network and arterial bus routes, and the inner ring road pass nearby.

A 'signature' tower and four low-rise atrium buildings are landscaped into a campus with wide tracts of public space. Three layers of basement conceal car parking. The 38-floor tower, Bavaria's tallest building on completion, is slender, maximizing the use of natural light with full-height glazing to the external walls. The plan could not be more efficient: a square core, stepping back in three tiers up the building, is surrounded by open floor-plates spanning onto 24 perimeter columns. The external envelope is the same on all faces, but the internal organization orientates itself north–south. As the building rises, the core gives way to internal columns and, at the very top, a double-height space is incorporated. The structure achieves maximum efficiency, both in terms of material use and simplicity of construction. The core of reinforced concrete acts as a

Above left: A reinforced-concrete frame braced by a central core of services and circulation is enclosed within a glass and aluminium skin.

Above right: Each part of this speculative office block – structure, envelope and services – is reduced to its essence and then refined in every joint and detail.

Right: The tower is free-standing within a campus of landscaped office accommodation. Simplicity is the only imposing feature of the glazed pillar.

cantilever to provide all the lateral stiffness and wind resistance the tower requires. Formed with standard climbing shutters it supports the inner edges of the reinforced-concrete floor plates, which are ribbed for lightness and cast on reusable table forms (metal trestles that can be quickly lifted up as the building rises). Prefabricated steel perimeter columns, relieved of any bending by the central core, are of minimal circular cross-section, set inboard of the slab edges and rapidly fixed within the shuttering as construction proceeded. The deep car-parking basements take the building down to an adequate formation, relieving the ground below of some of the new weight being applied and allowing the foundation to be a simple reinforced concrete-raft, 3.5 metres (11 feet) thick, cast rapidly between sheet-steel retaining walls.

Loadbearing elements are kept away from the building corners so that the façades can wrap smoothly round the building and over the cornice line. The slick skin and rounded edges of the building reduce wind pressure and drag across the face of the building. Noise levels are minimized and down-draughts prevented. The façade comprises single-storey-height panels, fixed to the slab edges with adjustable brackets to overcome the tolerance difference between the cast-concrete edge and machined seams of the cladding. The external joints have double seals. Due to wind drawing air out of the permeable building, the internal pressure tends to be lower than that outside. A double seal, in which the space between is allowed to leak and equalize with the external conditions, prevents water being sucked inwards. The inner barrier protects the outer joint and allows it to perform.

Double-glazing the wall provides a good degree of insulation, against both heat loss in winter and gain in summer. Coating glass can improve performance significantly. In cold conditions, the inner face of single-skin glass façades tends to be at a lower temperature than the rest of the interior surfaces, giving a sensation of draughtiness towards the window. A low-emissivity coating (such as a thin film of metal or oxide) on the inner surface of the outer pane of double glazing allows short-wave radiation (sunlight) in, but stops long-wave radiation, coming off warm surfaces within, from getting out. The inner pane of glass warms up to a comfortable level and overall insulation performance is improved. Reflective finishes economically reduce excessive heat gain and glare.

The most interesting feature of this building's envelope is in its provision of ventilation. Circular hopper vents are dispersed across the face of the building providing localized, infinitely variable, natural ventilation. The self-contained units are let through the centre of the glass panels. Their flange seals are simple, proven to high pressures and readily inspected and repaired. Automatic sensors control small actuators in the reliable mechanism. This pragmatic use of tried and tested technologies in new combinations, economically producing elements of extra capability, can only encourage the further development of fully responsive façades.

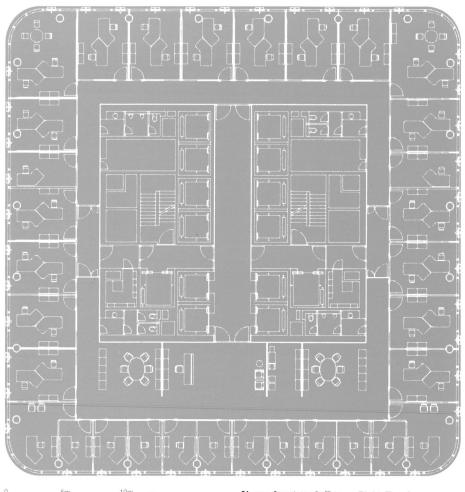

0   5m   10m
15ft   30ft

Above: A variety of office accommodation can be arranged around the open floor space. The central core steps back as the building rises, giving deeper plan areas on the south side at higher levels.

Right: The glass wrap does not vary around the building. Localized venti-lators are distributed across the outer surfaces.

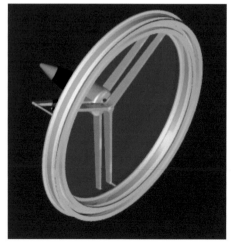

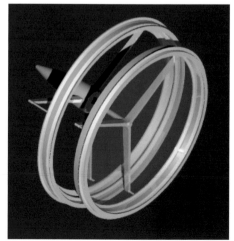

Top: Localized ventilators on the outer surfaces respond automatically to conditions within the immediate vicinity.

Above: The self-contained units are easily maintained and replaced. The failure of individual units does not significantly impair the overall behaviour of the façade. The opening is easily adjustable, from the barest leakage to the entire area of the circle.

Right: The structure sits on a rigid raft foundation shaped to reflect the pattern of imposed loading. Basement walls were installed from ground level before digging commenced.

BUILDING	BERGISEL SKI JUMP
LOCATION	INNSBRUCK, AUSTRIA, 2002
ARCHITECT	ZAHA HADID ARCHITECTS
ENGINEER	JANE WERNICK/
	CHRISTIAN ASTE

Amongst the ever-increasing range of Olympic sports, Nordic ski-jumping remains uniquely spectacular. Its extreme specialization has concentrated excellence in a small group of countries, where the challenge of the hills has become a source of national prestige.

In 1809, the Tyrolean freedom fighter Andreas Hofer turned back the invading Bavarians on the slopes of the Bergisel mountain above the Inn valley. The site, clearly visible from the city of Innsbruck, was subsequently appropriated by the locals as the location for national and international competitions. Anyone who has seen the New Year 'Four Hills' tournament, now televised worldwide, will recall the start box's outlook over the beautiful city to the Nordkette mountain range beyond, and the jump's alignment on the Willen Church and cemetery, directly below.

The first ski-jumping competitions date back to 1927, when a natural jump was improved with earthworks to become the

schanze or rampart – the Austrian word is still used for the approach track with its connotations of artificial landscape, conflict and fortitude. In the 1930s, a design was prepared by the engineer Horst Passer for a spare, functionalist, modern structure in reinforced concrete. The access tower and runway were abstracted from the surrounding wooded slopes. War intervened, however, and the building itself was not constructed until 1949, becoming one of the major centres for the sport in subsequent years and acting as the 'large hill' in the 1964 and 1976 Winter Olympics.

Sporting standards rise, and international competition surpassed the old jump. As part of a larger refurbishment project for the Olympic Arena area of Innsbruck, a competition was held to find a replacement structure – mixing the highly specialized requirements of the competition with public spaces, and a café and viewing terrace. The winning scheme is an architectural monument, clearly reflecting the dynamics

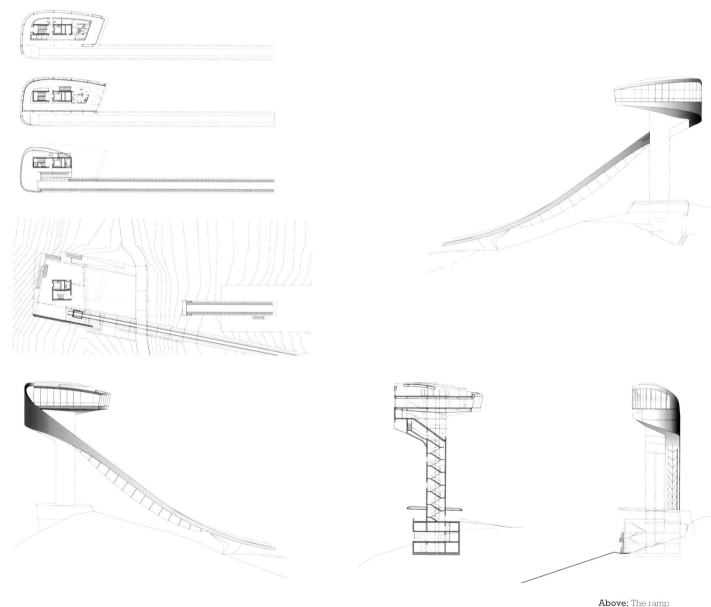

Above: The ramp comprises a bridge suspended between tower and base abutment. A catenary cable supports the lightweight deck in its ideal profile.

Above: The smooth
sweep of the metal-
framed run is carried into
the steel skeleton of the
tower pavilion. The
lightweight superstruc-
ture bears on a transfer
plate and supporting
shaft of in-situ concrete.

of the sport. The architect's declared intention was to 'intensify the landscape', combining the different programmes into a single new shape, 'extending the topology of the slope into the sky', and maintaining the idea of a landmark on the city's skyline.

Replacing Passer's sports apparatus with these post-Modern sensibilities, the structural scheme adds a tension, separating the access tower, observation enclosure and restaurant from the bridge-like jump itself. The ramp, swept of snow, is subject to the very lightest of loads – the lone competitor – and its parabolic shape has been exploited as a hanging strip, suspended between solid elements to make a very thin band against the skyline. The trajectory the jumper makes is not quite the ideal structural curve – so a light triangulation is added, to manipulate the shape and add stiffening, both vertically and horizontally, to the metal decking. Sheltering parapets on each side of the run attract wind load, and the bracing beneath the deck becomes correspondingly heavier. The structure is made relatively flexible, as deflection and vibration limits are less onerous than for other built forms. No one, after all, will be out on the run in high winds.

The ends of the jump are substantial reinforced-concrete abutments, and there is a dissonance between the main tower and the lower pier. The base block angles forward to form the lip of the jump, and simultaneously resists lateral loads from the ramp attachment; a perfect structural form. The upper termination is extended into a wrap-around, melding into the accommodation cantilevered off the vertical stem of the tower. Overall, the form expresses competitors' movements at the expense of structural logic.

Above: The upper part of the ski ramp extends around the tower as a wrap-around. The ramp itself is made to be relatively flexible.

The reinforced-concrete structure is monolithic and was cast in situ using climbing formwork, the material used here without engineering nuance to realize the required volumetric composition. Distributed steel reinforcement within the cement-and-aggregate matrix enables good-quality concrete to resist the harsh environment. Weathering like an artificial stone, the material eventually spalls in the frost. Keeping water off the surface of the building becomes the critical detailing concern, and the handling is little changed from Passer's day. Water is channelled off spandrels, and 'drips' are added to prevent it blowing beneath soffits. The 'viper's head' of accommodation is clad in a screen of profiled metal, into which a glazed curtain-wall is mounted. Rain beats against the outer surface, which is not fully sealed. Air pressures within the cavity between metal and concrete stay the same as those outside whatever the wind, and, within the sheltered gap, water is not blown inwards.

The stem of the tower carries two lifts rising from a funicular railway, bringing skiers and spectators up the mountain. The base of the pylon comprises a block of accommodation sunk back into the mountain. The basement matches the shape of the tower platforms above, and carries the loads of the building through the weathered material overlying the mountain's rock core. The empty volume replacing the excavated material ensured that the slope of the existing mountain was not overloaded by the new buildings, triggering a landslip.

The project's lighting design is subtle. Small projectors are dispersed, and concealed beneath parapets so that visible light is almost all reflected – reducing contrast, and avoiding far-reaching light pollution detracting from Innsbruck's towering new landmark.

Above: The upper works and ramp are integrated into a single form by an overall metal cladding. This rainscreen protects the weather-sealed envelope from snow and wind.

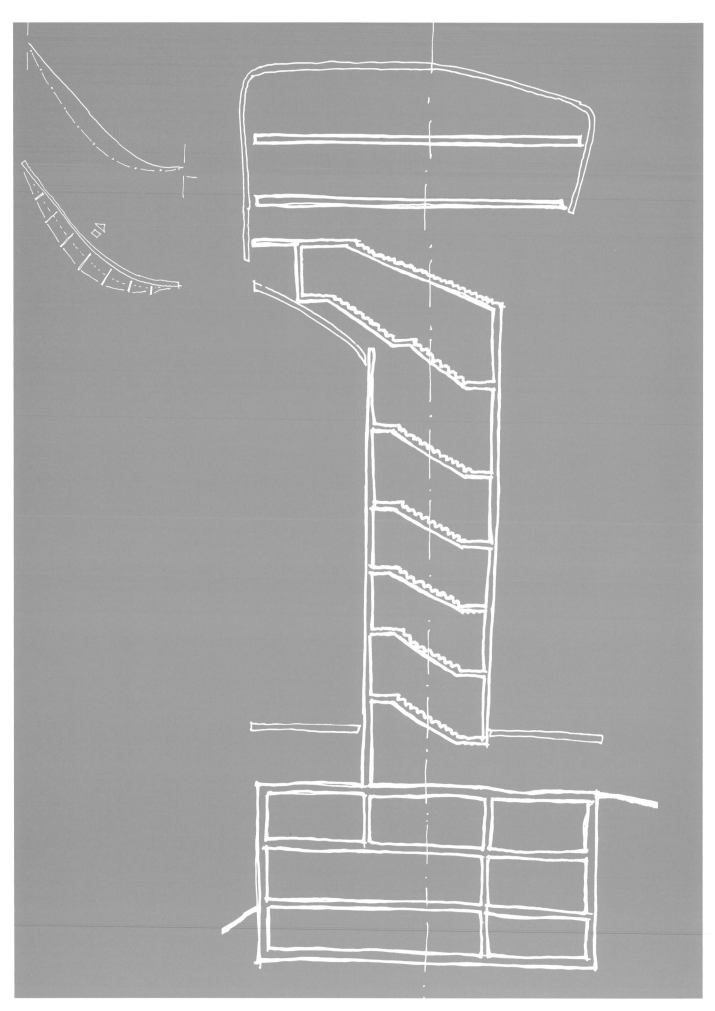

Above: The basement structures minimize the loading applied to the existing slopes. The differing curvatures of run and catenary create a simple cable-truss.

108

Above: The structure of
the observation platform
is suppressed behind
a neutral skin of glass
and steel cladding.
Heavy mullions resist
high wind loads.

BUILDING **TWIN TOWERS**
LOCATION **VIENNA, AUSTRIA, 2001**
ARCHITECT **MASSIMILIANO FUKSAS**
ENGINEER **BÜRO THUMBERGER
+ KRESSMEIER**

The city of Vienna, underpopulated since the end of the Second World War, is now expanding rapidly, bearing the brunt of an influx into the European Union from the old Austro-Hungarian possessions to the east. Set on the edge of a workers' residential quarter on the southern periphery of the city, and next to a greenbelt below the Vienna Woods, the Wienerberger Twin Towers embody a series of subtle solutions to the problems set up by demographic change.

Offices and a shopping centre (that most banal of programmes), and the large-scale intrusion into mature surroundings, are addressed with a simple organization of layout. The bulk of accommodation is divided into two towers, identical externally, placed over a city-block-sized podium set to the height of the surrounding streets.

A sinuous country-road form inserted between the two slab blocks sets up a picturesque relationship between the two. The accommodation is interconnected, with bridges springing from the short end of the west block into the centre of the long side of the eastern one.

The cladding of the office towers is simple: full-height glazing comprising a thin double-glazed skin, coated on the inner face of its outer panel to reflect away solar heat gains and glare. Daylight and vistas across the city and surrounding hills are maximized. When viewed head-on from outside, one sees straight through the walls of each tower and out the other side; when seen from a slant angle, the surroundings and sky are reflected off the building's face. The angulation of the two towers makes one

Above: The building is conceived as an artefact on a border with nature. Structures within the podium are differentiated from their surroundings.

Right: Similar in proportion and structural framing, the two towers are linked by bridges. These must allow for each system to sway slightly independently in the wind.

110

translucent and one opaque from any standpoint, and a third 'virtual tower' is implied in the reflections.

Proportion and detail are carefully handled. Each panel of the façade repeats the motif of the entire block. Mullions and transoms are suppressed to flush, neutral joints. Each pane is factory-bonded into a high-tolerance aluminium frame, so-called structural glazing where the glass actually adheres in place on a silicon bead rather than being mechanically fastened back. This envelope runs on above the roof of the building to terminate without a cornice of any kind. The high rain-water run-off from this smooth impervious system is easily picked up, as the two vertical blocks connect onto the roof of the podium below with no separation of any kind. The podium roof area is not colonized with air extractors or cooling towers, but kept uncluttered. The bracing patterns minimize movement from wind and temperature change between the two sides of the building. Provisions for sliding joints and bearings under the bridge links are simplified.

Despite the external match, internal layouts vary significantly. The lift, staircores and risers, and main bracing elements are arrayed longitudinally in the west tower, to suit cellular office plans. The eastern block carries vertical circulation on its two ends, suiting either cellular or open-plan 'office landscape' floor plans.

Structural arrangements are common to both towers: simple reinforced-concrete framing of 34 floors. Circular perimeter columns at close centres support nominal downstands, which stop the uprights punching through the very thin floor slabs. When pulled back slightly, these beams carry the weight of the glass skin as it passes by, avoiding any interruption to the state of even tension apparent across the faces of the buildings.

The slanting geometries are carried through the base structure, all the time reinforcing a sense of 'urban landscape' – the idea that there is a natural sub-order beneath the artifice. Tower and podium buildings conventionally incorporate a

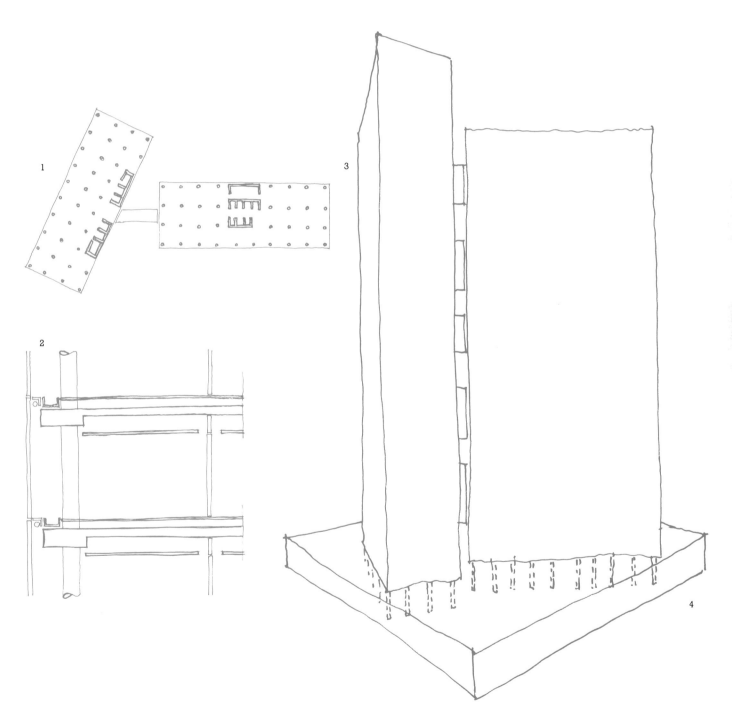

Left: Tower blocks and window-panes are carefully proportioned together. Reflections and transparencies are subtly manipulated in the placing of the two prisms.

1. In order to reduce movement across the bridge-links, the cores of the two buildings are organized to maximize their stiffness parallel to the bridges' axes.

2. The external envelope of the building is detailed to visually suppress the slab edge, and to incorporate blind boxes and perimeter heating to reduce wall draughts.

3. The loadbearing elements of the twin towers are carried down through the podium levels without the intervention of expensive transfer structures, redistributing the pattern of structure.

4. Lower levels of accommodation are organized around the forest of columns dropping through from above on two conflicting grids.

113

transfer structure at the junction between their vertical and horizontal elements, which channels vertical loads around the major spaces at low level. In this project, the tower columns carry through, with large auditoria set alongside, to make animated circulation and foyer spaces. Arcade rooflights frame views of the slabs tower forms above. The architect evolved these intermediate spaces, and their permeation with the incidental, around a phrase on which the project and its relationship to the surrounding city was supposedly grounded: 'What is happening in between?'

The scheme retrieves virtues from its economies: structure, cladding and construction are all conventional, taken to their rational limit. As the headquarters of the Wienerberger building materials company, the project is meant to demonstrate the continuing potential of established building materials.

Reinforced concrete is traditionally slower to erect than steel framing. Chemists have developed new mixes that can be made to harden rapidly and gain strength, but stiffness still takes longer to develop. This building was completed at a competitive speed, using special 'back propping' techniques. Temporary struts were left within the newly constructed skeleton for a considerable time, so that the building could rise apace. The soft frame was effectively held up within a temporary frame until it became strong enough to support its own weight and resist wind loads.

Fully developed systems for structure, envelope and servicing are combined in this building into an architecture in which the designer claims to capture 'transition, connection and transparency – because the city is energy and tension'.

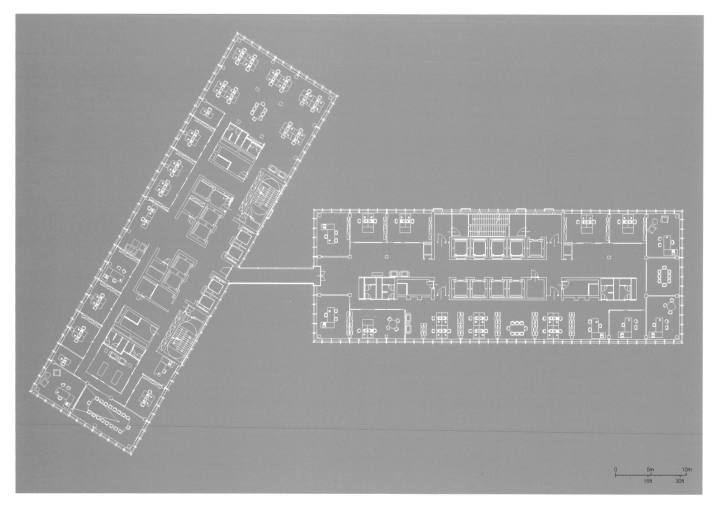

0   5m   10m
15ft   30ft

Above: The simple framing pattern common to both blocks is varied by the bracing provisions. Lift shafts and core-walls occupy the less well-lit areas of the configuration.

Right: Lamping levels are generally reduced to limit light pollution at night. Interactions across the wall planes multiply the patterns of point sources, breaking down bulk and profile.

BUILDING	MONTEVIDEO
LOCATION	ROTTERDAM, THE NETHERLANDS, 2005
ARCHITECT	MECANOO ARCHITECTEN
ENGINEER	ABT

Ideas of high-rise living and working have always met with a mixed reception across Europe. Paris has exiled its towers beyond the Périphérique ring road, and the City of London is only just opening the floodgates to skyscraper development. In Rotterdam, an experiment is now under way to make a distinctive tall-building type reflecting European aspirations and sensibilities.

Montevideo is a mixed-use complex comprising predominantly residential space, with offices, shops, and health and sports facilities appended. Branded part of a complete 'lifestyle concept', it is marketed as a completely self-contained environment, offering a continuity of living, working and nightlife. The site is an upmarket location in the Rotterdam regeneration area, called 'Maasstad'. Here, at the tip of the Kop van Zuid – an island in the Maas Estuary – there are views out to sea; back towards the city and its famous bridge, the Erasmusbrug; and around to the Rijnhaven, the biggest dock area in Europe. The project takes its name from an old warehouse, long gone from the wharf, which once received goods from the Uruguayan capital.

The architect, Francine Houben of Mecanoo, characterizes her approach to design as invoking 'contrast, composition and complexity'. This avowal sits well with the ambition to create a place sufficiently rich in diversity to fully sustain the urban 'good life'. The ambiguities and potentials of the site, poised between sea and land, are there to be addressed and exploited. The built form – tower and podium block – is developed as a series of interlocking blocks, crossing and closing around one another to make a balanced composition. These divisions reflect the provision of various accommodation types. In the central sections, loft units are given high ceilings; 'water apartments' cantilevered out over the river offer views upstream. On the west end, the tower has a lower section of 'city apartments', conventionally planned dwellings, while the top 15 floors are given over to 'sky apartments' with loggias and sliding screens opening out onto the views. New York-style water towers, with conical roofs on stilts, emphasize that the building is to be read as a variegated city block rather than a homogeneous entity.

The highly rational structure follows and reflects this diversity. The lower 27 storeys of the tower comprise reinforced-concrete cross-walls and floors, a system perfected by

Above: The high-level apartments are framed in steel to provide open-plan living areas and panoramic windows.

Above: The variegated envelope of the building reflects the diversity of accommodation within. Old-fashioned water towers and a chain-link roof enclosure recall traditional urban living.

the Dutch to provide cheap residential accommodation. This element is lifted off the ground plane on a steel trestle and then surmounted by a multi-storey steel frame, which reduces weight and allows for the wide, open wall treatments at high level. The remainder of the tower is concrete-framed, with steel elements appearing wherever necessary to assist in the wider spans or in cantilevering elements. The whole complex stands above a steel-sheet-piled basement enclosure made within the reclamation of the surrounding Wilhelminapier. The weight of the building is carried by nearly 700 driven piles, carried down through the soft alluvium of the river mouth.

The sales motto for the scheme is 'dressed for living', and the building's elevations are veneered on in recognition of potential occupants' preferences. Conventional flats are cased within brown masonry walls with punched windows. Other units are wrapped in smooth metal cladding. Lofts open out with full-height windows, which display their interiors as much as they open out to the surroundings.

Provision is made for all the flats to be controlled automatically, with a computerized management system regulating heating, lighting and sunblinds so that comfort and energy consumption need not be completely compromised by the increased window areas. The large number of junctions set up by this mixture of structure and cladding type is handled expertly in the construction planning. Prefabricated steel-framing and panellized cladding systems are assembled at very high speed, and much ingenuity is exercised in making the concrete work keep up. The cross-walls of the tower are erected using jacked forms. These progress well ahead of the floors, to spread out activity. Storey-height precast-concrete panels front and back enclose the apartment spaces, to allow finishing to commence as early as possible.

Despite its size, the subtle treatment of massing and surface makes Montevideo a well-mannered neighbour. The huge, neon-lit letter 'M' topping out the structure ensures that this experiment in high rise will not go unnoticed.

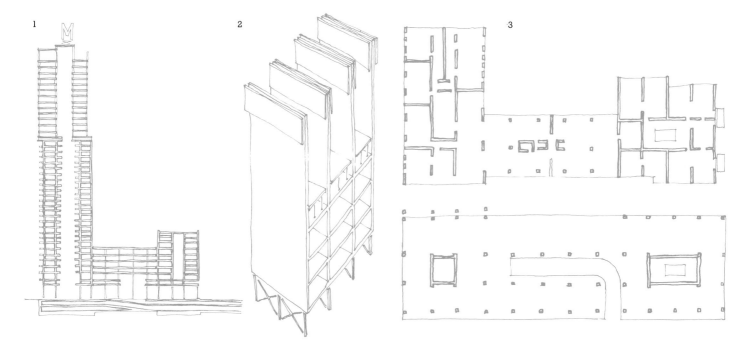

1   2   3

1. Steel-framed 'sky apartments' rest on the reinforced-concrete cross-walls of 'city apartments' to make an efficient and strong tower.

2. Construction time was minimized by casting the cross-walls ahead of the floors. The concrete in vertical elements had time to harden before being loaded.

3. The floor layouts of the tower and adjacent accommodation are set out on a simple grid aligning with the car-parking basement. Expensive transfer structures are avoided.

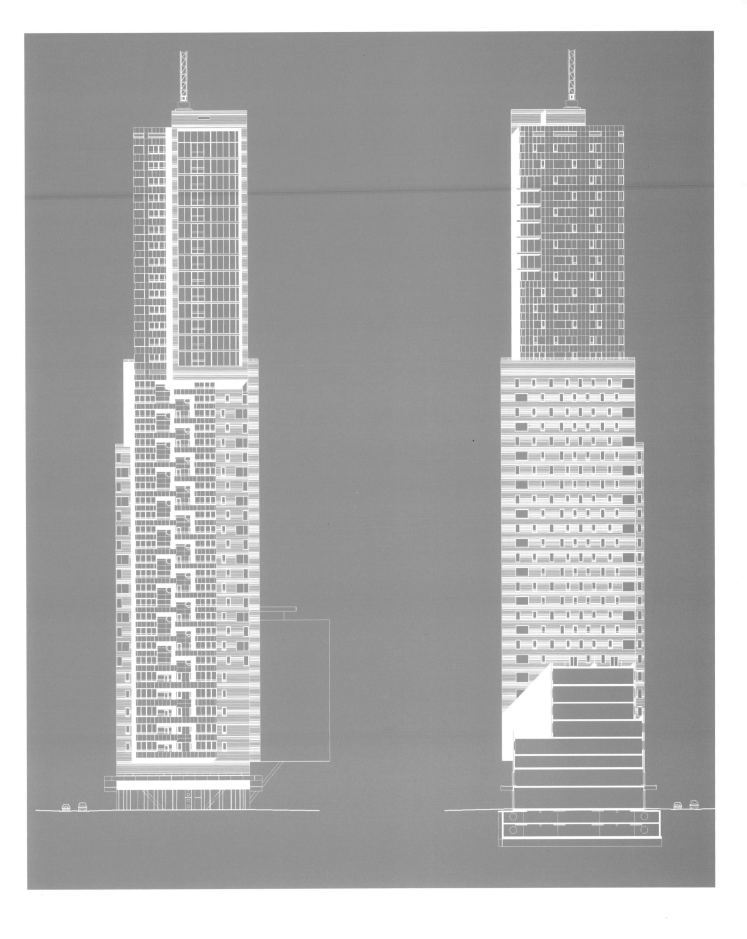

Above: The open frame of the upper storeys is emphasized by curtain walling. The heavyweight outer walls below have fenestration whose size and shape correspond to the living spaces within.

Above: The waterproof box of the basement is set in an old wharf on the River Maas. It is prevented from rising out of the surrounding groundwater by the weight of the building above.

BUILDING   **TURNING TORSO**
LOCATION   **MALMÖ, SWEDEN, 2005**
ARCHITECT **SANTIAGO CALATRAVA**
ENGINEER   **SANTIAGO CALATRAVA SA**

The Copenhagen-Malmö conurbation – linking the Scandinavian countries of Denmark and Sweden, across the separating strait, into the Øresund district – incorporates many significant initiatives in sustainable urbanism. The Danish capital itself is supplied with electricity from the Mittlegrunden offshore wind farm, and the giant bridge crossing the straits was designed to have no environmental impact whatsoever on its immediate surroundings. In the western harbour area of Malmö, on contaminated land left over from redundant shipbuilding yards, a regeneration initiative now centres around the construction of the largest residential tower in Sweden.

Situated within walking distance of the town centre and nearby Ribersborg beach, the accommodation is mixed: two lower cubes contain offices; the upper seven, 152 apartments. Guest suites, public function rooms and a wine cellar are communally maintained. The contorted shapes generate a variety of flat layouts, their free plans swept sideways by the slanting windows. Space planning was undertaken by a local firm of architects. In this way of designing, detailed planning becomes uncoupled from the overall preoccupation with form.

The tower's structure combines a strong, elementary aesthetic with an environmental design agenda. The building is treated as one of the architect's celebrated model experiments, writ large. Assuming the mantle of artist/architect/engineer, Calatrava has published widely a series of finely tuned sculptural studies: geometric shapes balanced on fulcra. Coupled with a personal

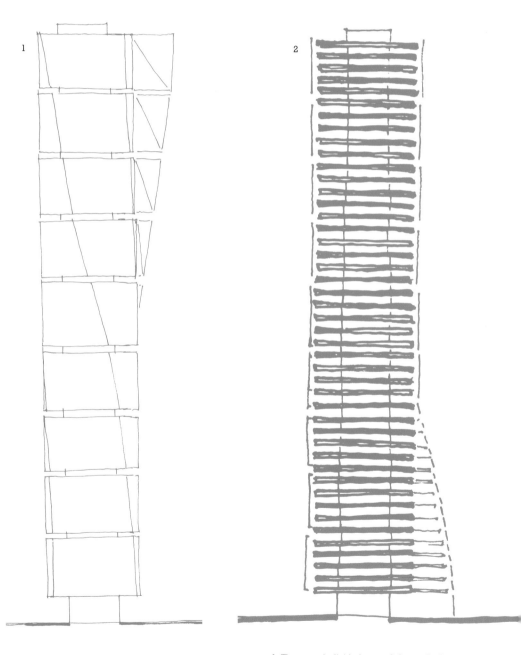

1. The tower is divided vertically into distorted cuboids twisting upwards through a quarter turn. A spine appears to tie down the balanced masses.

2. Internally the structure comprises a stack of floor plates supported on a central core. The triangular extension is propped up at the back corner.

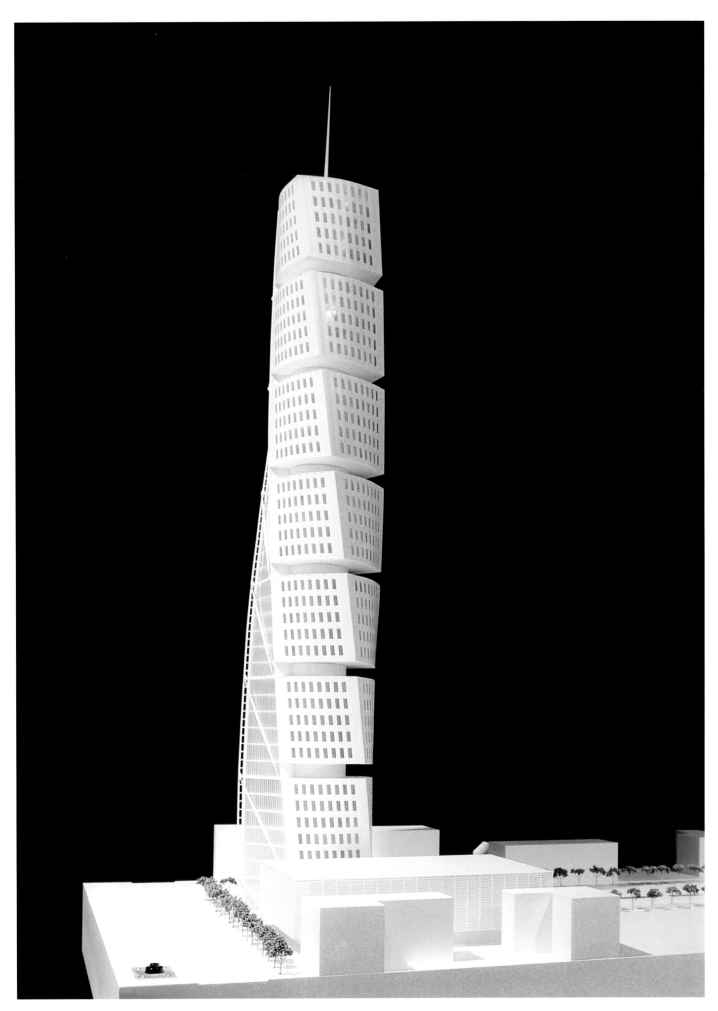

Above: The segmental expression of the building is achieved through the cladding. Each storey is supported locally on the slab edges so gaps can be opened at any level.

regime that includes life drawing in the morning and design work in the afternoon, his underlying interest in anthropomorphism translates directly into this project. Nine accommodation blocks, of five storeys each, spiral upwards around a circular core, twisting 90 degrees across the 30 floors of the building. Elevations and window openings are distorted to follow this movement. On plan, the rectangular shape of each block is opened out and given a triangular 'tail' with glazed sides, giving the impression that the giant cubes are balanced by a braced spine. This is an almost literal interpretation of classical figure drawing – particularly its mannerist variant, which treats the human form as an assemblage of blocks twisting, wedging and locking. The presentation for the project is even fronted by a watercolour sketch of a reclining figure

in conventional life-drawing pose.

The structure, however, is a hybrid – not at all what it seems. The circular central core, conventionally formed in concrete, carries lifts and risers. Floors cantilever outwards, independently of one another so that the 'twist' can be imparted without generating an extraordinarily onerous load pattern. The triangular spine of the building, off which the form might appear to hang, is, in fact, an appendage of the main tower. Triangulated braces, at the level of the lowest box, transfer loads from the spine back to the core. A post then runs upwards, which the 'tails' of the floors above bear onto and, in turn, restrain. The cladding is designed to differentiate the individual boxes.

The building's 'green' credentials are good. Non-toxic products are used throughout. Recycling and waste-management systems are

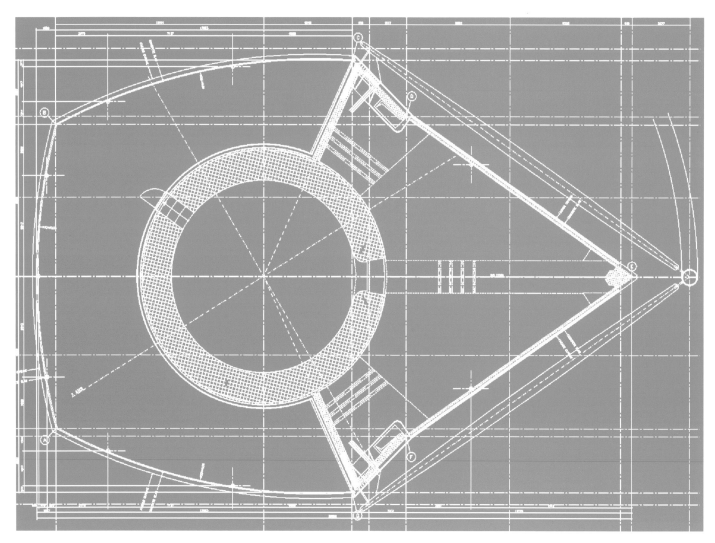

Above: A supporting core of reinforced concrete allows the free-form platforms to be turned at each level with no change of detail. The back section is decorated externally with truss elements.

fully developed, and a 'biogas' plant generates fuel for the city's buses.

The real interest in this building lies in what it is not. The tallest structure in Sweden, and set in the southern industrial heartland that has generated so much of the country's wealth in the past, the project has consumed much of the area's regeneration budget, and it remains to be seen if the return will justify itself. The construction has been costly, and yet does not fully embrace the innovation of the design's proposition. The shipbuilding traditions of Malmö – exploiting massive-scaled sectional prefabrication, developed in the Second World War and extended by the rig-building requirements of North Sea exploration – should have been able to provide real box structures. The weights involved should have made it possible to balance the box structures into the prevailing winds, restrained by high-strength tendons and held in perfect equilibrium by the restoring forces set up by the building's offset axes. The structural nodes would have become real nexuses of force, channelling and expressing the structure's behaviour, instead of decoration highlighted in the building's casings.

Tower configurations have not settled into a closed grouping, and this departure represents a new instability in what constitutes our understanding of tall buildings. It is a one-off, but with the possibility of a whole range of related configurations and extensions into buildings that are not mere point blocks.

The Malmö tower may eventually take its place as a precursor of future demountable systems. Many new buildings are designed superficially to be sustainable, reusing materials and more valuable sub-assemblies wherever possible. But the reuse of whole buildings really reduces the energy consumed and locked up in the built environment, and the possibility of complete relocation lifts this strategy to a new potential.

Another outcome of these experiments may be the development of a reconfigurable architecture. The architect Santiago Calatrava's designs have been justified as an aesthetic of movement, reconstituting static and dynamic approaches to form. More simply, they often act as studies for moving systems with their actuators omitted. Fitted with hydraulic cylinders, sensors and a very robust control system, the Turning Torso concept becomes a sunflower-tower, tracking the light or responding resiliently to the four winds.

Above: The cladding is panellized and mounted on chassis rails to make the best seals possible across the warped planes of the building.

Above: The massing and twist of the solid blocks are emphasized by regular punched windows sheared into parallelograms. The enclosure of the tail is suppressed within smooth, uninflected curtain walling.

123

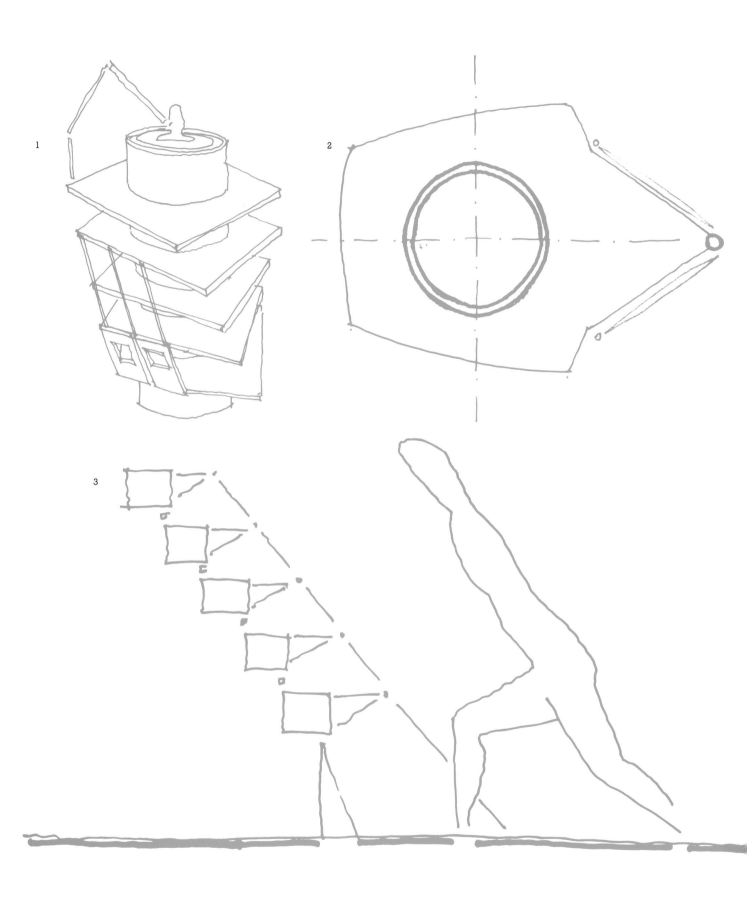

1

2

3

1. The reinforced-concrete structure was made with lift forms rising within the central core. A centrally placed concrete pump distributed material across the decks.

2. The angular envelope surrounding the circular core provides a variety of spaces to be laid out as customized flats. The segmental spaces are well lit from the external walls.

3. The anthropomorphic origins of the built form are recorded in the architect's sketchbook. Classical figure studies are juxtaposed with ideas for structural sculptures.

Above: A sculptural study of cubes stacked on fulcra. An attempt has been made to transpose the immediate appeal of this assembly's poise and elegance into a full-size tower.

BUILDING **STRATOSPHERE TOWER**
LOCATION **LAS VEGAS, USA, 1996**
ARCHITECT **GARY WILSON**
ENGINEER **BRENT WRIGHT**

In Andrea Dusl's essay 'Seven Towers' – an historical survey of the building type – she cites the Salt Tower on the Aussee Lake in Austria to illustrate a trait of outlandishness. Three years before Columbus discovered the West Indies in 1492, some deep foundations of an ancient Roman watchtower were uncovered along the old

salt road in the ancient Roman province of Pannonia in south-eastern Europe. The medieval multimillionaire Hans Hertzheimer, whose fortune was based on the salt trade, hatched a crackpot scheme to reconstruct the tower in an anachronistic design, 150 metres (490 feet) high, with a clock by Kepler set into the pinnacle. He

Above: Las Vegas by night. The height limitations imposed by the nearby airport prevents the Stratosphere Tower lifting off above its neighbours.

died, broken in wealth and health, with his project in hock to the Fugger banking family, in 1532. Construction had reached 7 metres (23 feet) above ground level.

The tower as folly has a long history. In Las Vegas, where dreams are a commodity, buildings can reach extremes of representation. Visitors can find an Eiffel Tower, a London Bridge and a Palace of Versailles along its gridiron streets. The Stratosphere Casino Hotel intended to make its mark by importing a version of Toronto's CN Tower: a parabolic spire mounting an observation deck and transmission antenna at its summit. The idea of building just a little higher than the original's 553 metres (1,800 feet) was quickly abandoned due to the glide-path constraints of the nearby Middleton Airfield. At just over 350 metres (1,200 feet) the final design fails to soar above its neighbour, but just overtops the real Eiffel Tower and claims to be the tallest tower west of the Mississippi. This epithet ignores the nearby BREN Tower, built on

Jackass Flats – the atom-bomb test site in Nevada – in 1962 to test for airborne radiation. (Las Vegas's famous air of unreality is not inevitably benign.)

The Stratosphere Tower closely follows the principles governing the design of its Canadian forebear. A reinforced-concrete stem, composed of three buttresses, supports a stack of circular decks framed in steel. Its parabolic profile, reminiscent of the trunk of a tree, reflects the idealized form of a free-standing tower. This desert tower resists mild seismic activity and high winds efficiently. Its narrowing shaft carries four double-decker high-speed lifts up its centre line, and then widens again to become a stylized holder for the high-level 'pod' containing 12 storeys of accommodation. These latter decks are enclosed in an inverted cone of curtain walling, decorated with diagonal trussing,

its mullions incorporating extra movement provisions in anticipation of the daily extremes of temperature. The outward inclination of the glass cuts down on glare and heat gain, and combines with dark soffit finishes to stop internal reflections interrupting the view. The daytime outlook across the valley floor, and night-time impressions of the 'city of lights', are fully exploited here by a revolving restaurant, cocktail lounge and outdoor observation deck above. The core of the 'capsule' is given over to conference rooms, shops and the inevitable wedding chapel. An external helter-skelter is mounted on top of the building, and other vertiginous rides are installed at a high level to tempt visitors. Plans have been laid to exploit the concrete pylon itself as part of a huge roller coaster, extending across Las Vegas Boulevard and the surrounding rooftops.

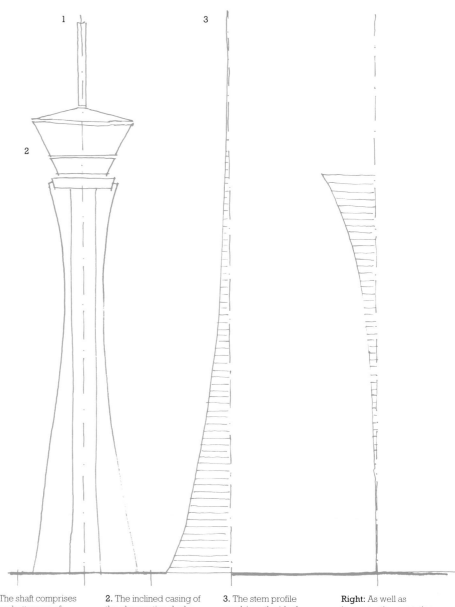

1. The shaft comprises three buttresses of reinforced concrete with a bank of high-speed lifts rising on the central axis. The upper platforms are framed in steel.

2. The inclined casing of the observation decks reduces glare and enhances the vertiginous views over the city grid and the valley beyond.

3. The stem profile combines the ideal parabolic shape of a free-standing mast with a top splay to support the substantial pod of high-level accommodation.

Right: As well as incorporating a rotation restaurant, bars and observation decks, the upper works of the tower hold a funfair and roller-coaster up to the desert sunlight.

The Russian film director Sergei Eisenstein first recognized the theatricality of large-scale building projects, and their potential for drama, referring to the 'choreography' of a pontoon bridge he was constructing on behalf of the 'Red' revolutionary forces. The drama of the two-year construction period of the Stratosphere Tower, a major intrusion in the city's downtown area, was exploited for its advertisement value. Rumours of set-backs, and technical difficulties, eventually overcome, may not have been discouraged and the construction itself had more than a hint of Eisenstein's theatricality. A very large climbing crane preceded the rising tower; on completion, a second smaller crane was fixed to the apex to dismantle the first mammoth unit; and then a third derrick was placed to remove the second crane. This last lifting equipment was finally derigged and carried off by hand, after a process lasting nearly four months. The structure was eventually crowned by a triangulated steel derrick, sized to be lifted into place by a so-called 'aircrane' or, rather, heavy-lift helicopter – the final attachment being signalled with a bright-red signal flare.

The resort city's life is principally nocturnal, and the lighting scheme for the tower combines an emphasize on the built form with restless movement. By the designers of the 'light art' along much of the 'Strip', a battery of xenon lights with varying colours emblazons the legs of the tower. The upper floors are picked out with several miles of LED lights, in strips programmed to 'pulse' and 'chase' so as to make the pod appear to spin. The rapid movements of the fairground rides in the building's crown are picked out, and further enhanced with stroboscopic lighting.

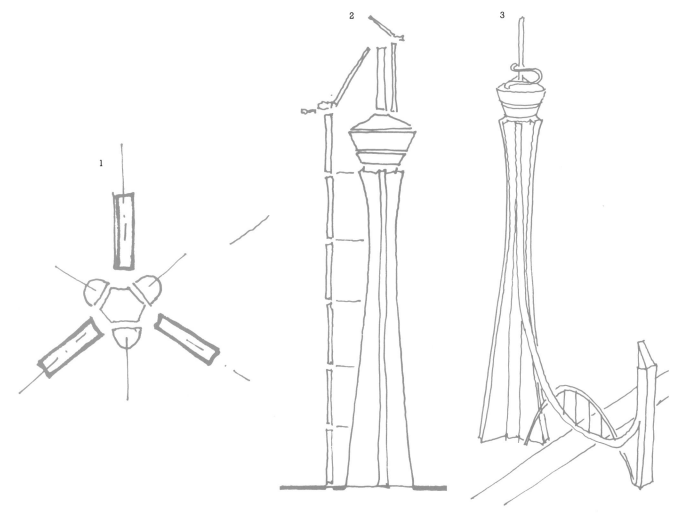

Left: Structural form dominates the design. A series of inessentials – bracket heads to the buttresses and cross-bracing on the pod – are pasted on.

1. Three supports opposed to one another at 120 degrees each is the most efficient plan configuration to resist lateral loads from any direction.

2. The construction phase of the project was dramatized. The climbing crane used during erection was dismantled by a perched crane which was in turn removed utilizing a temporary derrick.

3. Although the tower already carries spectacular switchbacks within its crown, a project is underway to incorporate the entire structure in an adventure ride of unprecedented size.

131

BUILDING   CONDÉ NAST TOWER
LOCATION   NEW YORK, USA, 2002
ARCHITECT   FOX AND FOWLE ARCHITECTS
ENGINEER   YSRAEL SEINUK

Number 4 Times Square, New York – the headquarters of the Condé Nast magazine-publishing group – is a concerted attempt by clients the Durst organization to build the world's most sustainable skyscraper. More than 80 per cent of the Earth's current resources are assigned to urbanism, and the long-term practicality and desirability of building high is at issue. The design team did not radicalize current practice but adopted a range of practical improvements influencing fabric, construction process and daily use.

The first speculative office block to be completed in Manhattan for over a decade, the 48-storey tower is the first of four in the West 42nd Street development programme. Times Square is just 100 years old with a chequered history but strong brand image, which the city and real estate interests have sought to rekindle. A move from the traditional publishing area of Madison Avenue was justified as a relocation to 'the crossroads of the world'. The building's form acknowledges its surroundings. Set on an interface between two of New York's highly differentiated downtown districts, it turns different elevations to different directions: an animated façade of steel and glass onto the entertainment centre around the square, a more sober composition of stepped-back volumes and punched windows towards the 42nd Street business area and Bryant Park beyond. The

organization of the steel-framed structure, central core and secondary perimeter columns is expressed at the top of the building and allows the development of the silhouette as a hierarchy of interpenetrating volumes. The building's role as link to the wide world is strongly emphasized. Super-scale signage advertises the building itself, and a corner tower of electronic signboards at street level brings breaking news to passers-by. The theatrical antennae array at high level signals the hard functionality of a communications station, visually tidying up the continually changing battery of equipment.

The embodied energy of the material employed – the amount of heat used and locked into the fabric as it was manufactured and put into place – was carefully audited and minimized as design and construction progressed. Recyclable parts, frame members and mass materials were logged. A second use can almost halve the energy losses of the construction process.

In a competitive speculative market full air-conditioning was always going to be the objective, and mechanical systems are accepted and made as environmentally efficient as possible. The building envelope is conventional, a state-of-the-art curtain wall with extra insulation and external shading to reduce insolation. Windows are larger than legal requirements, to make the most of daylight and minimize electrical

Right: The main frame-work of the tower is symmetrical and extended by subframes on each face. Each aspect of the building responds to the adjacent neighbourhood.

lighting. The plant runs on natural gas and the fuel burden is reduced by using efficient absorption chillers. Photovoltaic solar collectors in the brise-soleil on each storey supplement the supply, and two fuel cells are installed. These units act like batteries, retrieving energy from the mains gas supply by chemical means. With no burning there are no emissions. The air-delivery system provides 50 per cent more fresh air than industry codes demand, reducing the annual cooling loads. Variable-speed drives to fans and pumps are governed by a sophisticated building-management system. Sensors are distributed throughout the building – monitoring temperature, humidity, carbon dioxide, particle and contaminant levels. Computer controls calibrated by an extended commissioning process continually rebalance energy consumption across the building. A maintenance programme will

effectively recommission the building every five years. One of the major sources of energy waste in North America stems from large building systems falling out of synchronization, and so working against themselves.

The reduction of waste in all its forms has been a key objective of the entire project – in design, construction and use. Demolition rubble was crushed and recycled as aggregate for concrete. The substructure of the tower is surrounded by historic buildings, old subway tunnels and major utilities. Deep-rock caissons ensure that the weight of the building does not draw down neighbours, but existing structures, retaining walls and footings, were reused wherever possible – retained by careful planning and reloaded with a weight distribution designed to mimic previous conditions. Lift banks are effectively voids removed from usable floor area. A shaft-sharing system has been

introduced: a bank of lifts with more than one car per shaft is programmed to make the best use of resources from the movement requests it receives, and the volume of idle space is thereby reduced. Stringent management procedures reducing wastage were imposed during construction, an important factor in minimizing the building's embodied energy. Perhaps the least dramatic but most important of the project's initiatives has been the continuation of this control into the day-to-day operation of the building. A comprehensive set of tenant guidelines has been developed and instituted, with the management resources essential to its success. A network of recycling chutes is provided throughout the building. Air-conditioning can be locally controlled and tenants are provided with a plan to make their operations as energy-efficient as possible.

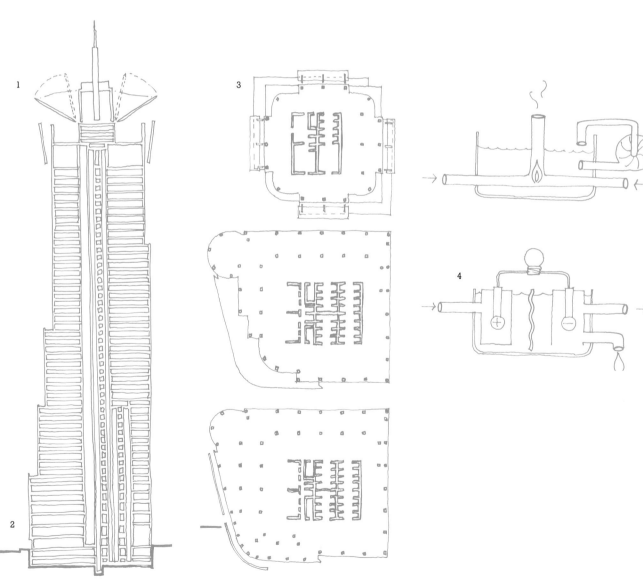

1. The structure is topped out with antennae and signage gantries symbolizing communication. Alterations and additions will not detract from the busy profile.

2. Existing ground structures were incorporated into the basement design of the building to minimize disruption during construction and reduce the costs of subterranean working.

3. Recycling chutes permeate the building. Circulation space is reduced by shaft-sharing; lifts and services are dispersed throughout the building to minimize riser spaces.

4. Fuel cells are one energy source for the building. Instead of burning gas, which produces heat and fumes, electricity is generated chemically, with water the only by-product.

Right: The corner of the building adjacent to Times Square is curved, and its cladding is streamlined. The podium supports an electronic signboard.

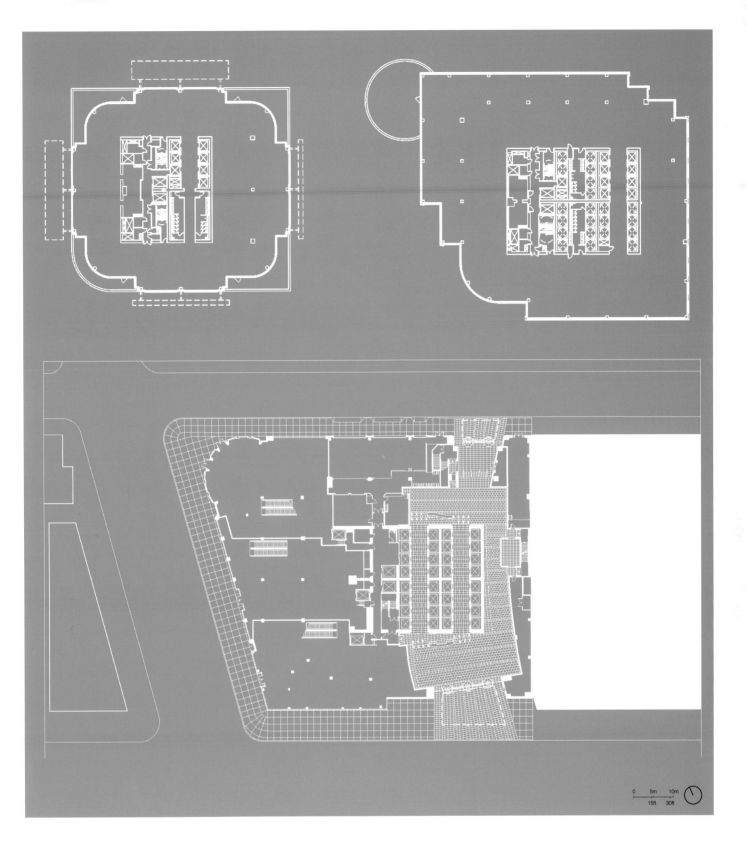

Left: The vertical segmentation of the towers relates in scale to the surrounding buildings, reducing the apparent bulk of the development.

Above: Clockwise from top left: Upper, lower and ground level plans. A regular trabeated steel frame fills out at the lower levels to completely occupy the site. At ground floor a full-width concourse returns space to the public realm.

BUILDING   NEW YORK TIMES BUILDING
LOCATION   NEW YORK, USA, 2004
ARCHITECT RENZO PIANO BUILDING
           WORKSHOP/FOX AND
           FOWLE ARCHITECTS
ENGINEER   THORNTON-TOMASETTI
           ENGINEERS

Dignified, impressive, inspiring and historical – these are the words most chosen by employees of *The New York Times* in a survey to determine preferences for the design of their new headquarters building. Here 2,500 people, dispersed over seven sites, are to be brought together in a landmark building. Shown the prototypes, they opted for a combination of simplicity, historical form, warm colours and materials, a mix of classical and modern motifs and, the report says, 'a spire shaped roof'.

Sixteen firms competed in invited competition. The winning collaboration – between the architects responsible for the Debis House at Berlin's new Postdamer Platz, and the engineers for New York's Condé Nast Tower (both discussed in this book on pp. 80–85 and 132–137) – synthesizes their respective preoccupations. Renzo Piano, the consummate building technologist retrieves the bland curtain wall, returning it to its correct incarnation as a highly engineered environmental buffer.

Above: The rectilinear building, reflecting the gridiron layout of the city, is transparent but veiled behind filigree screens of white ceramic rods.

Fox and Fowle's work promoting practical sustainability and minimal energy use is extended by detailed technical studies, including a 420-metre^2 (4,500-square-foot) mock-up of the building acting as an evaluative test bed for alternative technologies and systems.

It is difficult to win a major contemporary design competition without a strong rhetoric. The theme here is light and transparency, which models well. Lit from within, crisp acrylic surrounded by photo-etched filigrees in itself makes for a seductive presentation object. Computer graphics are particularly suited to rendering specular effects and translucency. Piano's manipulation of light – extending from the Menil Gallery, with its roof baffles softening the Texan sunshine, through the Hermès Building in Tokyo, whose glass-brick envelope is silvered within the joints to reflect the city lights, to the light-scattering screens of the Berlin Debis House – takes another turn here. In front of the transparent

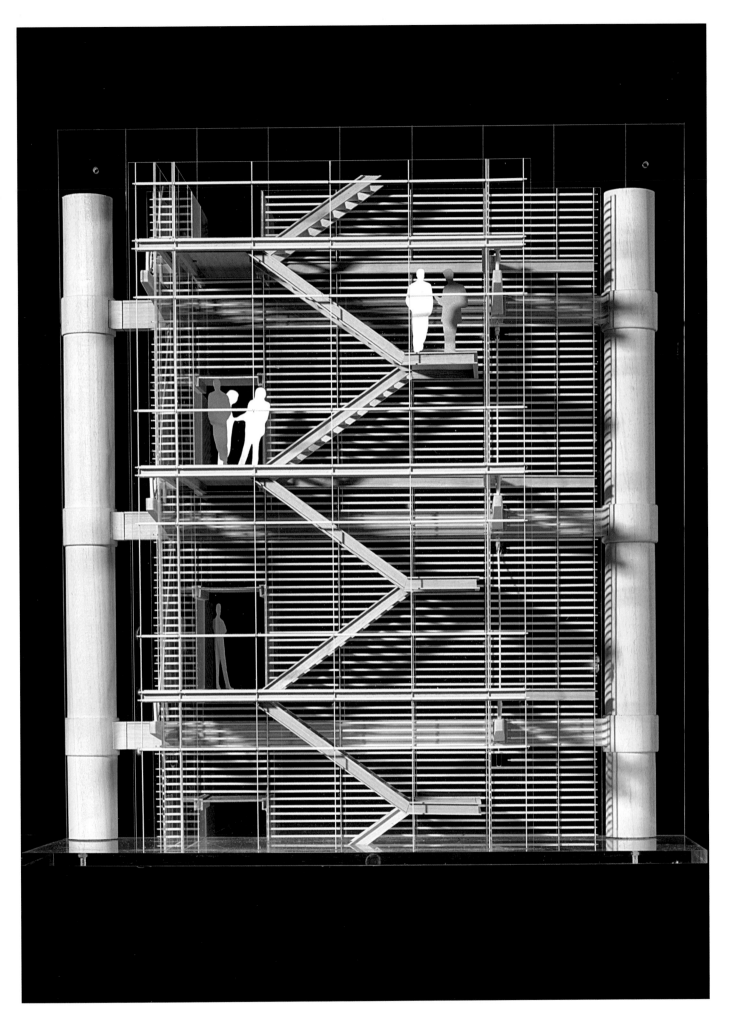

Above: Each corner
contains accommodation
stairs, encouraging local
movement between
floors. The screens are
drawn back and the stairs
are clear-glazed to
display this activity and
provide views outwards.

façades – double-glazed with the latest, 'spectrally selective', low- emissivity glass – he sets arrays of white ceramic tubing, reminiscent of Frank Lloyd Wright's Johnson Wax Factory. Cheaply extruded and assembled with the simplest of spigot joints, the panels create a subtle, weightless screening, reflecting light deeper into the building and reducing glare. Ceiling heights are generous and partitions stopped short to extend daylight penetration. No tinting or enhanced reflectivity is employed. The building takes colour from its surroundings – in the competition presentation described as 'bluish after rain, red at sunset', attaining a 'vibrancy' in the city's changeable atmosphere. The tower has been draped in a 'suncoat' rather than the raincoat of a traditional façade. The lower building is roofed with a reflecting water pool, and the building's openness integrates it into its surroundings. The four-storey newsroom at ground level ('the bakery' according to the

architect) is visibly frenetic 24 hours a day – connecting the newspaper directly to its source, the street. Occupying the entire block on the east side of Eighth Avenue between 40th and 41st Street, and anchoring the south-west corner of the Times Square redevelopment, this cool translucency is a strong reaction to the seediness of the adjacent bus terminus; the poor man's gateway to the city with its rows of blacked-out windows, peep shows behind.

The base of the building gives to its surroundings. A public garden, 350-seat auditorium with glazed back-wall, and museum of the paper's history, are set behind a widened piazza. The whole composition is rigorously rectilinear, very calm in comparison with the celebrated visual cacophony of the surrounding advertising billboards and the morass of post-Modern edifices in the redevelopment area. The architect refers to the nearby Seagram Building as an influence, 'the best

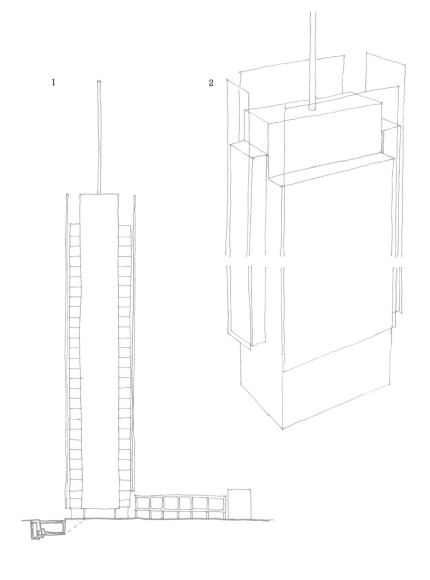

1. A carbon-fibre finial tops the structure out. Strong and flexible, the spire is designed to flex visibly in light winds without lashing in gales.

2. By raising the outer screens relative to the building enclosure the low-level newsroom is revealed to the street. Rooftop boardrooms and terraces are simultaneously shielded.

3. The clear glass façades and external screens of ceramic tubing, mounted on simple spigots, are neutral colours to directly reflect the changing shades of the sky.

4. The cylindrical screens are intended to diffuse glare and reflect light deep into the plan. Full-size prototype testing assists in achieving the best combination of diameter and spacing.

5. The screen-walls are interrupted locally, and the density of crossbars is varied, to allow views out across the city and down towards the streetscapes.

interpretation of the DNA of the city' – the gridiron plan of Manhattan, with its connotations of Dutch rationalism, and America's 'Protestant core'. Cross-fertilized with his regard for the 'romantic skyscrapers', the Empire State and Chrysler buildings, and their expressions of power, levitation and vibrancy, this approach enables Piano to respond to the brief's call for historical richness. The classically proportioned shaft of the tower is etherealized and animated by lifting the outer screening high above the street, extending it above the building and stopping it short of the glass stairwells on each corner. These ambiguous 'quoins' destabilize the perception of the building's form, blurring its boundaries. At roof level the screens thin out, protecting a grove of maples forming a quiet, contemplative space. The topmost storeys have a curiously retro feel, a sort of Gothic-tech Woolworth-Building effect. The spire has no communication function, and is just a wand capable of swaying in the wind, sensing the changing air currents.

Originally intended as just a furniture mock-up in a dark warehouse, a south-west quadrant of the building's typical floor has been prototyped in the grounds of the company's printing plant. With costs shared by the US Department of Energy and the California Energy Commission, simulations of entire years are being made to assess alternative hardware and control solutions. It is hoped that, as well as detailed specification requirements for the building, general findings will enable future research to be more specifically directed. The building industry might be stimulated to provide lower-cost technologies and systems that meet the needs of this building and then influence the wider market. The demonstration of new technologies in a landmark building gains them far more attention among manufacturers and specifiers than does the publishing of more conventional lab-based research.

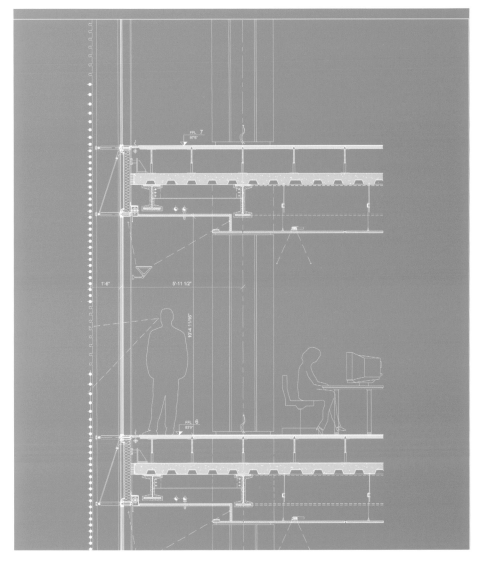

Above: The soffit section, floor to ceiling heights and internal partition system are all detailed to bring natural light as far as possible into the internal spaces.

Above: The profile of the building maintains something of the gothic filigrees of 1920s skyscrapers. The main frame is evenly distributed in slender columns behind the façades.

141

BUILDING   AOL TIME WARNER CENTER
LOCATION   NEW YORK, USA, 2003
ARCHITECT SKIDMORE, OWINGS
           AND MERRILL LLP
ENGINEER   CANTOR SEINUK

The new Time Warner Center on the south-west corner of New York's Central Park is an odd-looking building. This latest, most up-to-the-minute development in Manhattan is muted, seemingly pulled by conflicting influences. The opportunity for a big set-piece statement is bypassed in favour of an agglomeration of smaller geometries, addressing the building's immediate surroundings. This design has had a long back-story.

The scale of the project ensures it has a now traditional mixture of commercial uses. The Time Warner media company's headquarters is set alongside speculative offices, retail spaces and a shopping mall. A CNN television studio, the Mandarin Hotel and 225 condominium units are packed into a built form comprising podium-base and twin towers. Designed and modelled like a giant piece of furniture or a console, the complex conceals its disparate functions within uninflected forms and surfaces.

The project, now under construction, is the last in a line of proposals made to replace the New York Coliseum. Since the Second World War, Columbus Circle had become an increasingly seedy northern terminus to the city's theatre district. Robert Moses' bland Coliseum building – a venue sporting a huge blank façade of grey brick, set back from the interchange behind a windswept plaza – was opened in 1956 and was, almost immediately, universally, and sentimentally disliked. The opening of the Jacob K. Javits Convention Center nearby freed the site for redevelopment, but two decades of schemes were to follow – all meeting with objections from West Side community groups. Along the way, the mix of retail, commercial and residential uses was worked out and, at the mayor's instigation, a proposal for a jazz venue was introduced to the project. An extreme scheme proposal by Moishe Safdie, the architect of the Montreal Expo 'Habitat' Building, established the

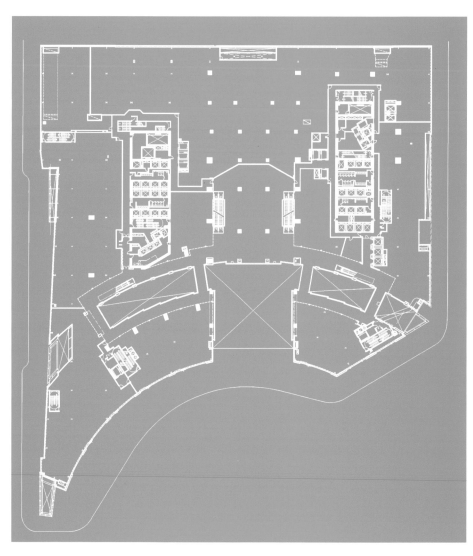

Above: The base of the mixed development fills the site with shops and arcades. Conventional steel-framing and composite steel-and-concrete slabs readily adapt to the variety of plan shapes.

Above: The twin towers and podium block are carved into volumes filling a space defined by sight lines, height limits, zoning regulations and the surrounding street plan.

143

Above: The low-level
elevations of the building
are scaled to address
Columbus Circle and
surrounding streets. The
towers are mirror-clad to
recede into the sky.

twin-tower concept. The scheme eventually steered through to construction embraces all these concerns.

The development is as big as is possible without overshadowing too much of Central Park. This was the critical issue generating the building's shape. Its form seems almost to have morphed over in a helioscope. The four-storey podium reaches forward to encircle Columbus's statue. The shopping mall opens directly through a glazed end wall onto this public space, albeit one choked with cars. The 'Jazz at the Lincoln Center' section of the project is inserted into the complex as a set piece designed by another architect, Rafael Viñoly, whose background portfolio includes the Tokyo Forum, a vast public-use building.

The external treatment of the towers proceeded through several transformations.

Safdie's busy, asymmetrical scheme became twin towers. Art Deco styling was discarded in favour of a plain Modernist curtaining. The strong bronzes and greens of nearby glazing was eschewed in favour of a pale blue, shown in presentation renderings strongly reflecting the sky and clouds. The top of the resulting building is finished with a pierced frieze; this pale imitation of the great heritage of Central Park West is a curious retro-styling, like the vestigial fin on a modern car. The motif harks right back to the 1922 Chicago Tribune Building competition, the occasion of an early paradigm shift in skyscraper design.

In this instance, technical expertise and an inclusive design process have not fused into an extraordinary outcome. There is an air of exhaustion in the result. The steel framing, detailed with rationalized joints for rapid and safe assembly, capable of carrying heavy masonry wallings as readily as light glass envelopes, is not a strong determinant of the design. Air-conditioning can make any space habitable, provided one turns a blind eye to energy consumption, and ensures that plans can be any depth. Construction pricing and whole-life costings are so confused that it remains difficult to rationally identify what is truly the best-value way to build. The pursuit of a sustainable expenditure of resources still rests largely on moral obligation. Only if a particular aspect of structure or servicing is focused upon, will it definitively inform modern building design.

The laxity of the basic design is disguised with details and finishes portraying quality. Areas and levels are demarcated to express social distinction, and a strict hierarchy of exclusivity is engendered. Tenants are sold

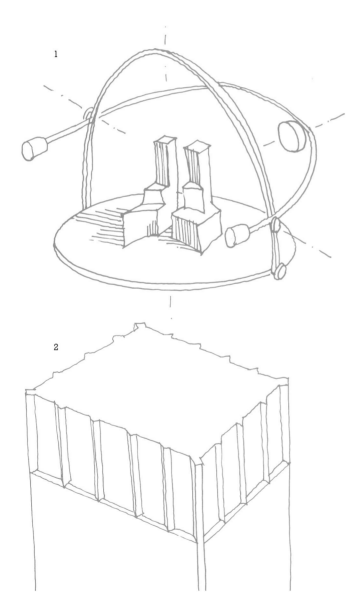

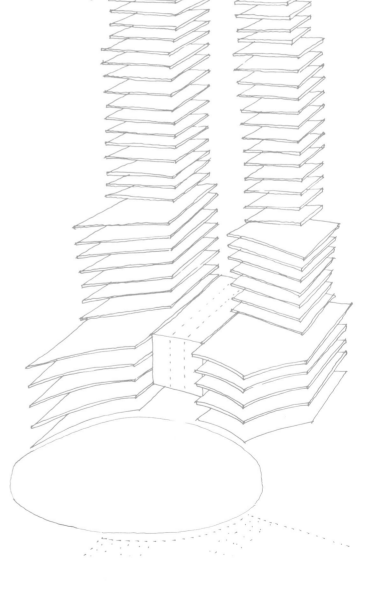

1. A heliograph traces the shadows cast by the design proposal. Computer models were made so that the building's silhouette can be manipulated to maintain neighbouring buildings' right to light.

2. The indented cornices of the towers employ a simple pattern of cladding using tried and tested corner junctions. The fluting catches changes of light.

3. The structure amounts to a stacking of floor plates on regularly spaced columns. Closer-spaced wall columns accommodate the shaped outer enclosure.

'lifestyle' in the form of special service provisions: according to the literature, in signing up one is 'buying every amenity imaginable'. This dislocation of structure from finishes and content may have had more than one origin. Behavioural patterns seem to require a surface readily 'branded' to the surroundings, and the construction of large buildings is naturally divided into sub-routines. It is easier both to imagine and manage packages of work by introducing conceptual as well as physical interfaces.

The long process of acquisition, one possibly involving more conflict than consultation, has also failed to produce a satisfactory compromise. Neighbours and residents, relieved that construction disruption is abating, remain unhappy with the resulting bulk and bustle. The profligate use of energy and materials embodied in the construction is open to continued criticism. For the occupant, the single entity dissolves into a township of places and parts. The designers have produced an innocuous building, a mild-mannered giant trying to make itself small and squeeze into the crowd. Perhaps big buildings need big ideals around which to shape themselves.

Above: A variety of spaces are packed onto the site. Large halls are set atop the podium freeing the ground plane for retail use and reducing structural weight.

Above: Layered façades and repetitive set-backs are adopted to reduce the apparent bulk of this huge building. The suspended screen to the central portico signals accessibility.

BUILDING HIGHCLIFF
LOCATION HONG KONG, 2002
ARCHITECT DENNIS LAU AND
          NG CHUN MAN ARCHITECTS
ENGINEER MAGNUSSON KLEMENCIC
          ASSOCIATES/MAUNSELL
          GROUP

This may be the tallest residential block in the world – outside the realm of commercial buildings, the title is not competed over. Perched high on the east face of the Peak in Hong Kong, this redevelopment of apartment towers on two adjacent sites has led, through an extraordinary set of conditions, to a pair of attenuated pillars set up in one of the worst wind environments in the world.

The territory has always set a premium on space. With no limit on height, and legislation designating a plot ratio of 1:8, accommodation to total area, the provision of high-specification flats is best resolved by piling double then single units to an unprecedented height. The acceptance of high-rise living has left 80 per cent of Hong Kong's ground plane open. Highcliff and its neighbour, 'the Summit', were under construction at the same time on behalf of two different clients, with one architect common to both designs. A comparison of differences and similarities is instructive – the scheme for the Summit following on from Highcliff.

The plans of both closely reflect their siting. The Summit has a clearly defined front and back, typical of Hong Kong housing, and faces north down Happy Valley. Its accommodation comprises pairs of two-storey maisonettes, and advantage is taken of the curving enclosures to expand space. Sited slightly higher up, Highcliff exploits the outstanding panoramic views on every side. An intersecting pair of ellipses generates its plan, which divides into two units around a central circulation core at low level and large single units above. Internal planning in the apartments of both buildings, however, is disappointingly orthogonal.

The external curves of the two pylons acknowledge one another, a composition of repose also avoiding the adverse energy irregularities of concern in feng shui, and minimizing typhoon loading. Both structures are in cast reinforced-concrete, ideally suited to making the free-form structural elements required. A cellular arrangement of cross-walls is tied to a perimeter pierced for windows but

Above: The curving form of the residential blocks is taken up in the interior decoration of the entrance foyers. The finishes include an illuminated glass staircase.

Above: The towers are supported on a deep reinforced-concrete transfer structure bearing on massive columns. The lower storeys are fully glazed to take in the view of the city.

strengthened with upstand beams and stiffening nibs to create rigid enclosing planes. The towers look astonishingly attenuated but it may be considered that they are scaled and structured like the central cores of the downtown buildings, which sustain all the lateral loads of much wider office complexes.

Concrete of inordinate strength is used to keep the volume of structural members from swamping the space planning. Stress designations of 100 N/mm^2 (14,500 pounds force/square inch) approach those of steel. As a construction material, concrete has several intrinsic problems: as it cures it heats up, baking cracks into itself; it shrinks over time; and it creeps very gradually under sustained loads. All these problems grow and must be addressed as greater strengths are called for. Great advances have been made in the past decade in the chemistry of additives, to improve the material's characteristics during moulding and in service. Sintered products such as silica fume make the wet mass more pourable,

Above: Two towers of extraordinary slender-ness are constructed using very high strength concrete. The underlying rock allows them very good foundations.

Above: The flamboyant interior design for the public spaces disguises the massive structure, uncoupling the column shafts and soffits from the surrounding surfaces.

149

avoiding segregation and loss of strength; other ashes create bulk, or aerate the mass to control internal movement. North American code standards were adopted by the Hong Kong City checking authorities to assess the structure's specification. Advances in non-linear computer analysis, predicting the behaviour of three-dimensional elements made up of materials whose characteristics change over time and which are flawed by a statistically generated pattern of cracking, mean that different imperfections can be modelled at design stage as a risk analysis of the proposal's sensitivity to the vagaries of the real world. The advances made in quality assurance procedures across the building industry have been essential to the safe deployment of such special materials.

Strength can be raised, but not the attendant elastic properties. Ductility of the structure – its ability to smear out local overloads and material inconsistencies – is not to be sacrificed for brittleness. It is accepted that movement will be just perceptible within the upper levels during storms. Dampers are installed to maintain comfort levels at all times. Sophisticated computerized electro/mechanical systems counteracting the building's every movement were passed over in favour of straightforward 'slosh dampers': interconnected water tanks drawing energy away from any oscillating build-up.

Highcliff's steeply sloping site is absorbed in classic Hong Kong fashion by bringing the towers down onto a deep transfer slab bearing on very large circular columns descending through a podium. This multi-storey block at low level is cut back into the hillside. Back-and side-walls are formed as

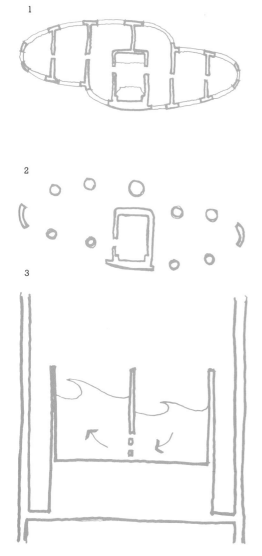

1. Configured like a bamboo stem, the main shaft of the tower is a multicellular tube made from the reinforced-concrete hull and cross-walls.

2. The lower levels of the building are structured with thick, squat columns acting with isolated cross-walls and central core to resist lateral loads by bending.

3. Buffeting from typhoons is absorbed with 'slosh' dampers in which a liquid mass is allowed to move and dissipate energy through friction.

4. The enclosing walls of the tower shafts are stiffened with sill beams forming horizontal rings at each level. Windows are carefully concealed behind a continuous glass cladding.

Above: The structure looks slender but is comparable to the reinforced-concrete core elements of modern skyscrapers. Shafts carry considerably higher wind loads.

Right: The elliptical profile of the building provides a degree of streamlining, reducing wind pressures and noise, particularly the whistling caused by sharp edges.

Above: Two flats per floor orientated towards the view define the form of the Summit tower. The podium block of car parking raises the lower units above the treeline.

Above right: The configuration of tower shaft resting on a deep transfer plate and column concentrations provides space for large volumes such as swimming-pools.

a palisade of large-diameter bored piles, retaining the surrounding ground down to a 3-metre (10-foot)-deep raft foundation excavated through the weathered layers to be cast straight onto the unfissured granite mass of the mountain. Floors brace the retaining walls, and transfer wind loads from the towers back to the surrounding rock. The nearby Summit found different conditions, and relies on an array of piles taken through to the bedrock.

The very high specification of the Highcliff building reflects the intention to rent in the volatile residential market. Life-cycle costing has permitted the use of very high-quality finishes. Real curved glass in the elliptical ends completes a sleek exterior of prefabricated panellized curved walling, shuffled into place and fixed from within to avoid fully scaffolding such a windy location. Joints are designed to remain watertight when the building sways during a typhoon. Full curtain-walling is unusual in residential development and the neighbouring tower uses much more common mosaic finishes and conventional framed windows. There are no wall-mounted air-conditioners – endemic in this city – but, instead, a fan-coil room is shoehorned into each apartment plan.

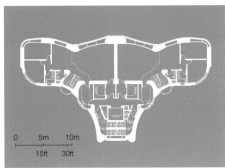

Above: The apartments are designed as two-storey units opening off a stiff spine of vertical circulation. Column thick-enings stiffen structural walls surrounding double-height spaces.

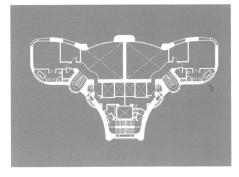

Above: The principal fire-escape stair, lift shafts and feature stairs linking mezzanines are all treated as stiffening elements within the reinforced-concrete frame.

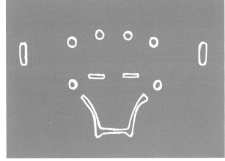

Above: The lower-storey columns are assisted by isolated cross-walls in resisting lateral loads. Efficient when widely spaced, these elements are set on the outer corners of the building.

153

BUILDING INTERNATIONAL
FINANCE CENTRE II
LOCATION HONG KONG, 2003
ARCHITECT CESAR PELLI AND
ASSOCIATES/ROCCO DESIGN
ENGINEER ARUP, HONG KONG

At its completion in 2003 the world's second
-tallest tower, Hong Kong's IFC II, also
occupies one of the world's most spectacular
settings. Its attenuated form rises directly
from the reclamation-land of Victoria
Harbour, to the same height as the
Peak forming its backdrop. The proportions
of the extremely slim 88- storey building are
activated by its relationship to a smaller
neighbour of a mere 38 storeys. The two
towers take their place in the famous
panorama of the city, just the most visible
element of a new city quarter and transport
interchange comprising airport terminal,
and mass-transit railway and ferry terminals
linking the island of Hong Kong to Kowloon
and the surrounding townships. At night –
in the peculiar 'lightscape' of Hong Kong,
frozen so as not to distract pilots landing
at the long-gone airport – the retro-styled
silhouette and futurist illuminations realize
the ethereal visions of artist Hugh Ferriss.

The armature of the ruched envelope
and tiered topping is a megacolumn frame.
Off a large reinforced-concrete core,
enclosing vertical circulation and risers,
each level comprises four areas of wide-
span floor spanning out to eight built-up
steel-plate columns of massive proportions.
These super-columns are concrete-filled to
enhance their structural capacity and

robustness. Every 20 floors, the two vertical
systems, columns and core, are tied together
with storey-height steel outriggers, to resist
typhoon wind loads. These outrigger floors
are filled with plant and fire-refuges, while
lifts and stairs pass right by. The corners of
the building, made up of re-entrants fluting
the building form and creating the corner
offices so sought after by minor executives,
are framed in a much lighter secondary
system carried down to a trussed-steel
transfer structure above the podium levels.

Mixing concrete and steel loadbearing
elements in such a tall building has its
problems. Concrete shrinks over time as
it hydrates and settles under load, whereas
steel is dimensionally stable. The differential
movements inherent in this design are dealt
with in the simplest way possible. The
junctions between concrete core and super-
column hull are packed with loose shims.
When the wind blows, the bearings
compress together and the system locks
up and acts in unison. If, during a yearly
inspection, the shims are found to be
permanently binding, due to the core
settling, then they are simply replaced with
thinner packers!

Sited on dredged silt dumped over
granite bedrock to build up dry land out of
the sea, the building's foundations employ

Above: The lights of
Hong Kong, frozen by
the old airport rules,
encourage the modelling
of built form using
'wall washers'.

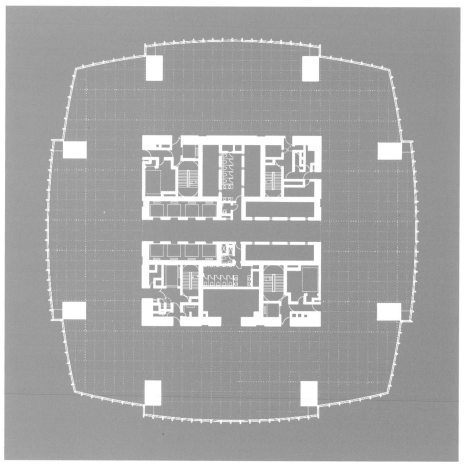

Above: The super-
column structure
comprises a substantial
core connected to eight
composite columns of
concrete-filled plate-
steel tubes surrounded
by lightweight secondary
framing.

Above: Rising straight up from the harbour reclamation, the attenuated tower reaches exactly the same height as the Peak, the famous backdrop to the city. The neighbouring tower emphasizes this tallness.

a sophisticated mixture of economy and practical construction. A deep circular trench was made, down through the reclamation silt to bedrock, using a boring machine automatically controlled to maintain line as it met uneven conditions in its descent. The unstable sides of the cutting were kept from collapsing by a filling of thixotropic mud (hard when undisturbed but softened by stirring), until concrete could be introduced by pump, displacing the overburden of mud. Reinforcing steel cages were dropped in from above and, upon hardening, the embedded wall was dug out from within to make a huge hole down to bedrock. The spoil was taken by sea to become the reclamation material for Hong Kong's Disneyland, out on Lantau Island. From out of the resulting pit, the building was brought back up off simple spread foundations made on the exposed and proven rock surface. Later on, as the surrounding basements began to be constructed, the circular wall was broken down and removed.

Hong Kong is one of the world's great water cities, and extensive use was made of the pier heads adjacent to the site for the removal of excavation spoil and the delivery

of building fabric. The link is direct to the worldwide market for building material. The building's steel framing was divided into a series of 'packages', contracts of a manageable scale which interlocked into a continuous procurement process. During basement construction, 1 million cubic metres of material was removed in 200,000 lorry movements, while 38,000 tonnes of steel framing was shipped in and 500,000 cubic metres of concrete was batched up on site. Design and construction work was organized into an overall programme, bringing construction materials to site at the exact time designated for assembly, without the need for storage. Steel came from many countries: Spanish in the basement, British in the transfer structures, Nippon steel and Chinese material higher up. As a trading centre, Hong Kong has no related market to which it is obliged, so its buildings reflect a truly global outlook.

The three-year construction phase of the project had a life of its own. Up to 3,500 individuals were engaged on the work at any one time, and safety, health and welfare provisions were rigorously detailed. There was a fire during construction work, always a concern with packaging material

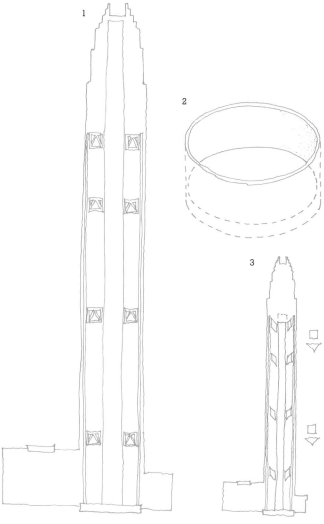
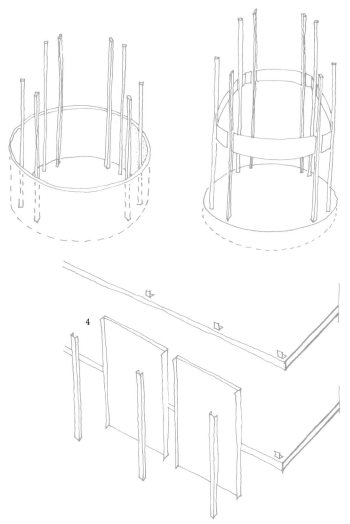

1. Typhoons create high wind pressures over the island. The tower's lateral resistance is enhanced by coupling core and mega-columns with outrigger floors.

2. Construction was speeded up by creating a temporary cofferdam in the reclamation, out of which the new structure could be rapidly raised without prolonged groundworks.

3. Concrete creeps and shrinks over time. The differential movement between core and frame is compensated for by removable shims on the outer ends of the outrigger cantilevers.

4. Individual cladding panels were lifted by crane and fixed at each slab edge from within. Pilaster strips ensure a good weather seal against the high winds.

Above: An early phase
of construction with the
circular retaining wall
cutting down to bedrock.
The frame for the bridge-
link taking ferry
passengers towards the
city is already in place.

157

everywhere and in this case workers cooking illegally at high level. Its prompt control proved the contractor's commitment to safety on site.

Modern building construction becomes a risk-management exercise, and methods are chosen to reduce hazards and mitigate the consequences of accidents and inevitable errors. Mixing concrete and steel construction, a cost decision, generated a major interface between two trades, and a corresponding potential for inexpediency. Concrete elements take longer to assemble than steel. In-situ work requires the construction, placing and adjustment of a mould; then formwork; then the installation of reinforcing steel; and finally concrete poured, compacted and allowed to set. Steel, by contrast, goes up stick by stick, very fast, provided the base to which it is fixed is within tolerance. The concrete core of this building was made to keep up with the surrounding steel hull and floors by using jump forms. A hydraulic lifting system raised massive steel-panel sides into which prefabricated steel cages were placed; concrete was poured and then, as soon as possible, the forms were 'struck' and leapfrogged upwards to a new position,

and the process repeated. Once set on their way, the forms are self-contained and the concrete can be pumped to position. Lines and levels were readily checked and corrected. Steel inserts, set into the walls as work proceeded, offered an instant interface with the surrounding structure following close behind. A faster system, using continuously moving formwork sliding upwards, (slip-forming), was not employed, being prone to progressive deviations, missed-out insets and inconsistent concrete work. Crane time is also a critical part of the programming. Only so much lifting capacity can be crammed into such a confined site area. The main frame progressed at the speed allowed by the craneage provided.

The IFC II was a speculative development, a brave endeavour in the volatile land market of the territory. The difficulties of constructing such a huge building in a confined city centre like Hong Kong's were compounded by the imperative for speed of assembly. Once the process of development, with its vast concentration of resources, is initiated, the accommodation has to be brought 'to market' as soon as at all humanly possible.

Above: The central core was cast with lifting shutters and a central platform jacked up on the completed work. Pockets were left in the walls for the frame to follow.

Above: As soon as the superstructure had cleared ground level the temporary bund was removed and excavation commenced on the transport interchange beneath and around the building's base.

Above: Core structure, steel frame and cladding packages follow one another upwards during the construction phase. Climbing cranes and external hoist systems lift materials and workers.

BUILDING **DI WANG COMMERCIAL CENTRE**
LOCATION **SHENZHEN, CHINA, 1996**
ARCHITECT **K.Y. CHEUNG DESIGN ASSOCIATES**
ENGINEER **LESLIE E. ROBERTSON/ MAUNSELL**

This tower and associated complex were built as an overt symbol of the spirit embodied in the new town of Shenzhen, southern China. Fuelled by a headlong industrialization of the former Canton and a deeply ingrained inferiority complex towards neighbouring Hong Kong, with its unique set of post-colonial values, the city has set out to turn – within one generation – from a subsistence farmers' village into a commercial centre and enterprise zone of six million souls, to match Shanghai and nearby Kowloon. The new building on 'Di Wang', loosely translating as 'best plot', is just 10 metres (33 feet) higher than I. M. Pei's masterpiece, the Bank of China Building in central Hong Kong.

The Cultural Revolution ended in 1976 and four years later Shenzhen was designated a Special Economic Zone (SEZ), a contact point for trade and information exchange with the outside world. Overseas Chinese investment and expertise returned to this new frontier and a building boom began. To bring a benchmark of quality to this process a landmark scheme for a mixed-use development in the city centre was let by international competition in late 1992. Completion was called for in April 1996 to pre-empt the return of Hong Kong to China in the following year. At the time, the country had no building code governing super-high-rise building. Privately funded, the development was to be a speculative venture comprising international-standard apartments and flexible office space divisible into the smaller units favoured by companies attracted into the SEZ. City authorities set no height limit in seeking a civic symbol. Addressing these aspirations, the design team applied well-tried construction technology and management practices imported through nearby Hong Kong, a familiar use for China's century-old 'window to the West'. The project became, de facto, a national training project, with hordes of officials and related professionals visiting to appraise the process. Lessons learnt were disseminated throughout the country, fulfilling the promise made by the creation of the SEZ.

Above: The distinctive profiles of office tower and residential block are brought together to dominate the city skyline. Decorative features are applied to straightforward structure.

Above: The long
slab block is concrete-
framed. Deep transfer-
girders allow for the
cut out. The slim tower
comprises a steel outer
hull linked to concrete
shear-walls.

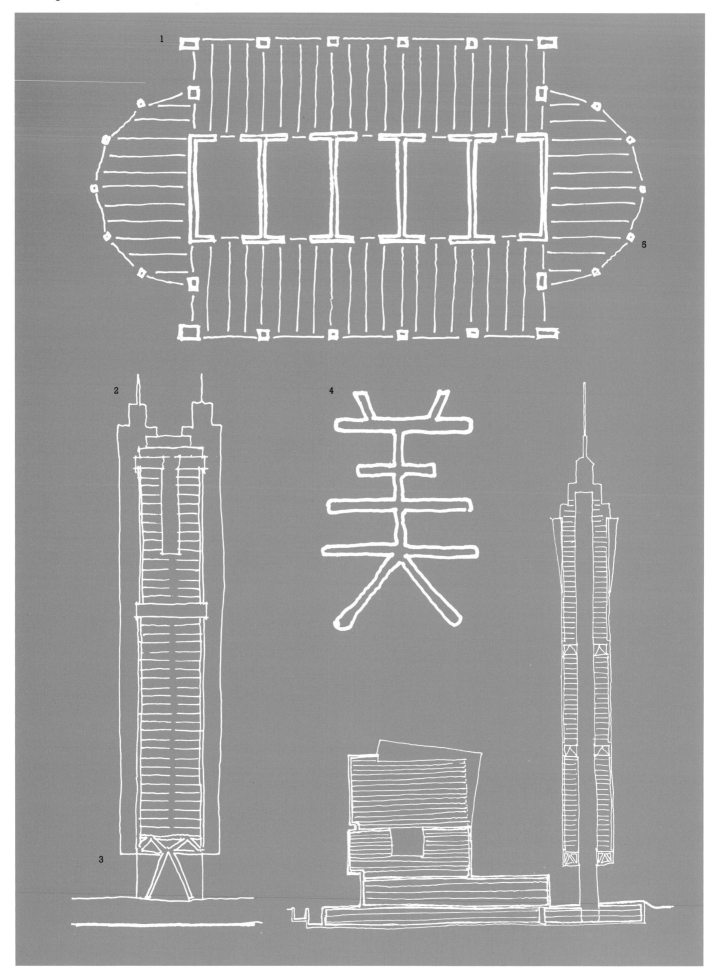

1. Corner columns extend beyond the slab edges, setting the side walls forward of cylindrical ends. The re-entrants formed in the façades conceal service risers.

2. The twin turrets, avoiding the bad-energy focus of a single finial, form an extensive compound for cooling towers and access gantry parking.

3. The main frame is supported on trussed girders spanning foyer spaces. A large A-frame braces the structure down through the entrance hall.

4. The modelling of the tower façades recalls the Mandarin character 'mei' which means 'beauty'.

5. Concrete-filled plate steel megacolumns act together with the large core to brace the building. Secondary frames form the cylindrical ends.

The timetable for handover forced the structure up very fast. It reflects all the expertise globalism can assemble. There has been no time for any kind of technical 'quarantine' to allow an indigenous expression to develop. The purchase of foreign specialization has been avoided by encouraging Chinese nationals, educated and settled abroad, to return with their experience and knowledge base. Initial designs for the winning entry to the competition were prepared from the architect's base in Berkeley, California. Once accepted, he promptly came to China to implement the construction. The design bears a remarkable consistency and simplicity through this compression of process.

The long narrow site, surrounding road network and indifferent townscape generate a straightforward site layout. Underground car parking is served by spiral ramps at each end, between which a shopping mall is laid out on axis, focusing on an old tree: a southern Chinese evergreen fig. New planting, of brightly flowering native kapok, is arranged in terraces around the development. Onto the podium of retail spaces and office accommodation two blocks are arranged: a tall office tower and a lower residential block, set at right angles to one another to avoid overlooking and to make the most of daylight.

In dealing with seismic conditions and typhoon loadings, the structure incorporates all the received knowledge guiding modern construction on the Pacific Rim. The predominance of a small range of methods is instructive. Most importantly, using familiar methods enabled the project to be completed without accident by a workforce that was gaining experience. The mall and residential block are in reinforced concrete. Simple, robust and insensitive to minor site malpractice, the material is labour-intensive and now deeply ingrained in the way the local building industry works.

The tall tower is very slender, combining a concrete core and steel outer hull and floors. This combination is widespread

Above: The development occupies an awkward triangular site. Access to the car-parking basements, through two spiral ramps, determines the setting out of the two main buildings.

163

along the Pacific Rim. The walls of the vertical circulation and risers resist the high wind loads and inertial forces of an earthquake. The steel surround provides flexible column-free space. The steel frame was developed in a competitive situation between the international consultancy Maunsell Asia and Nippon Steel, a Japanese manufacturer – a process intended to reveal best practice. Hong Kong engineers, led by the very experienced designer George Gillett, brought Australian expertise to bear, while the Japanese worked through the heavy steel – which came to be the concrete-filled – super-columns, making the corners of the main frame. The architect's conception of the two long walls as screens delimiting the building is reinforced by the re-entrants formed behind these column cores. Service risers are concealed within these rebates.

The Western preoccupation with corner offices as status symbols is missing here. Without overtly responding to feng shui, the rounded ends of the building cannot focus geo-energy or provide perches for malign influences, and they resolve the discord of the angled road-grids around the site. The curved ends are carried up to a distinctive paired finial; small pavilions contain coolers and window-cleaning plant. The twin forms suggest 'eye contact' with the city below instead of the aloofness exuded by tapering tower pinnacles, and the building is saturated with symbolism. As well as typically post-Modern motifs, most noticeably the tilt of façade elements transposing the triangular ground plan into the elevation and a key stone device splitting the top of the form, Chinese forms are everywhere. Edges are de-structured by ribbon-window banding wrapped around the corners. This patterning is reminiscent of the traditional 'Kung Fu' jacket. The green colour of the heavy typhoon-resistant glass façade represents prosperity. Serendipitiously, the building form reads as the Mandarin word 'mei' – beauty. Is the link the origin of the ideogram, a large mild-mannered presence, or a literary expression surfacing in such a quick design made without precedent?

Above: The structure is expressed in the entrance by cutting back mezzanines and inserting rooflights to separate principal elements from their surroundings.

Right: Externally, the walls, structure, canopies and fittings are cased in behind a panel system. Individual elements disappear behind the close jointing.

BUILDING	TAIPEI FINANCIAL CENTRE
LOCATION	TAIPEI, TAIWAN, 2004
ARCHITECT	C.Y. LEE PARTNERS
ENGINEER	EVERGREEN CONSULTING ENGINEERING

The island of Taiwan is one of the most active tectonic zones in the world. The weather report in Taipei's daily paper appends a section on 'yesterday's earthquakes'. Severe typhoon conditions and weak geology complete a catalogue of bad conditions in which to construct high rise. As the centrepiece of the new Hsingy financial and government district the beleaguered country has constructed the world's tallest tower, 502 metres (1,650 feet) high: a temporary epithet, soon to be passed to Hong Kong's Kowloon Harbour Centre – already under construction as the Taipei building topped out.

The structure incorporates massive resistance to lateral loadings, sufficient strength to resist the inertial forces produced by a 1-in-950-year earthquake – an occurrence of millennial rarity but one nearly met in the '921 Chi-Chi' event of 1999. Here, a megastructure concept is rigorously carried out in detail. A multicellular core of braced steel, becoming massive reinforced concrete shear walls below seventh floor, is coupled to a perimeter of eight 'mega columns' with 'megatruss' outriggers at every eighth floor. Within these box-like cells secondary frames support office decks of load-reducing

lightweight concrete on metal decking, and façades of special, low-emissivity coated glass – essential to controlling heat gain in Taiwan's strong sunshine.

The building's perimeter flares out below the 25th floor, buttressing the bulky shaft. Adjacent low-rise buildings separate out wide-span auditoria and retail spaces. The strong structural form is used expressively: each group of eight storeys flares out, evoking a pagoda form. Chinese symbolism makes the upfolding petal styling – a sign for prosperity. The raking surfaces are lit to create a floating lantern effect after dark.

The design of the components and structural details are all developed to add to the overall robustness and stiffness of the building. The giant perimeter columns are boxes of 80-millimetre (3-inch)-thick steel plate, filled as work progresses with super-strength silica fume concrete. Steel fins and studs key the two materials together to make a ductile whole: even if the frame were bent beyond recovery it would still go on absorbing energy and staving off collapse. Major joints are made by welding, blending the metal into a continuous skeleton of resistance. The cores are generally rolled sections but the 'mega-elements' require fabrication from plate, resulting in the

incorporation of an equivalent of 1,800 kilometres (1,120 miles) of weld lines. The column sizes – 2.4 metres by 3 metres (8 by 10 feet) – are determined not so much by strength requirements as by access considerations; operatives working within had to join components preheated to 100°C (212°F) to make the metal fuse properly. These joints had to be readily accessible and repairable. The other consideration controlling the size of structural element employed was the lifting equipment available. The megaframe concept became practicable with the availability of lifting capacity provided by the large climbing cranes that were originally developed for the oil industry. The volumes of the composite columns are governed by the quantities of concrete filling that can be lifted and placed.

The pinnacle at the top of the tower, taking it into the record books, sustains some of the highest wind loads a building can be subjected to. Vortex shedding, rhythmic eddying in the shaft's wake, is inevitable and the weld details are carefully made with smooth corners to survive the fatigue of

an extraordinary three million stress reversals over the life of the structure.

The stiffness achieved in the frame takes the natural frequency of the structure, its resonance, very high, almost beyond the level of human perceptibility. To enhance the building's static resistance to cyclic loadings a huge steel ball-damper is inserted at the 88th floor. Weighing 650 tonnes it is formed by a pendulum of welded plates attached to an array of viscous dampers, and counters any energy build-up from loads fluctuating near the natural frequency of the tower. A significant earthquake during the construction period was always anticipated, and this adversity was turned to advantage. Sensors were set up to measure the partially completed building's response and the information gained was then used to re-calibrate the computer models used in the dynamic design, to correct assumptions, and to adjust the equipment installed. The damper becomes a feature, visible from the observation deck and rooftop restaurant.

The soil conditions of the city, 60 metres (200 feet) of soft silty clay overlying firmer

cemented sand, only serve to aggravate earthquake shocks. The foundations of the new building are massive, more than 380 piles cast deep into the sands then tied together with a mat foundation sharing the load into the weaker upper layers. Five levels of basement mitigates some of the additional loading.

Elastic shortening in the very long piles and sands is expected to sink the building and its immediate surroundings by about 35 to 55 millimetres ($1\frac{1}{2}$ to 2 inches). The finishes are then adjusted to account for this drawdown. The structural analysis necessary to predict the gradual shortening and movement of the structure was extended to assess the vulnerability of the partially completed structure, at all major stages, to an extreme earthquake or wind event. Sadly in March 2002 a Richter scale 6.8 earthquake, (Kobe, January 1995, was 6.9) shook two of the climbing cranes off the 60th floor, killing the operators and three others. In the endeavour that is construction nature's dangers can be mitigated but rarely precluded.

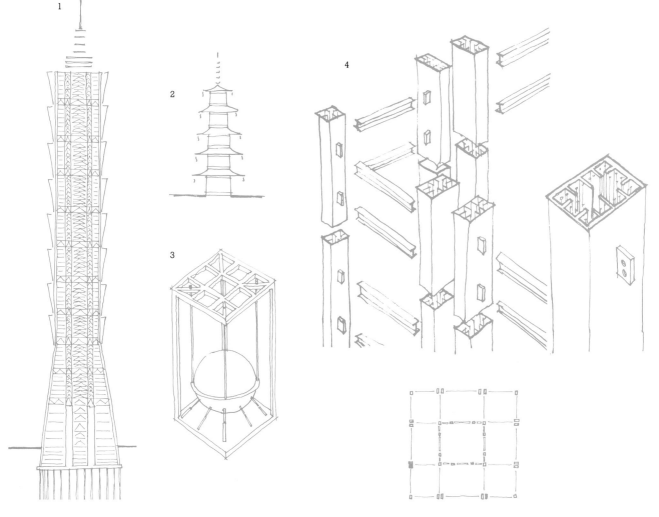

Previous page: The tower under construction is a township within itself. The temporary access gantry is sized to deliver several thousand tonnes of material.

1. Built in one of the most seismically sensitive locations in the world, the structure is made stiff with a steel-braced core and massive concrete buttressing in the lower levels.

2. The traditional pagoda is structured to resist seismic shocks. Each tier vibrates differently; an effect lost in this design.

3. A tuned mass damper, comprising a huge metal pendulum-bob surrounded by hydraulic shock absorbers, features in the upper works.

4. Extensive use is made of the megacolumn concept. Fabricated tubes of steel filled with concrete are doubled and joined to the strongly braced core cage.

Above: The lighting scheme emphasizes the structure's tiered form. Strong uplighters on each corner are concealed behind the ledging and divide the form into weightless segments.

BUILDING	PETRONAS TOWERS
LOCATION	KUALA LUMPUR, MALAYSIA, 1997
ARCHITECT	CESAR PELLI AND ASSOCIATES
ENGINEER	THORNTON–TOMASETTI/ RANHILL BERSEKUTU

Can buildings ever become too big? What will check the relentless increases in building height? It seems that European and North American cities can no longer take the disruption of the very biggest re-developments. As the twin Petronas Towers took over from the Chicago Sears Tower as the highest buildings in the world, competition seems to have moved to the 'Asian tiger' economies of the Pacific Rim. Perhaps local social structures are more capable of adapting to the intrusions. Philosophies recognizing life's flux may encourage a more frenetic urbanism. The Petronas Towers are part of a complex generating over 170,000 square metres (1.8 million square feet) of usable space. Transport infrastructure and compensatory external spaces are left to catch up with the new establishment. The competition brief to find a design for the project specifically demanded a treatment reflecting the culture and climate of Malaysia. The success of the winning scheme's response can be judged by how much more than skin-deep the building is: it is informed by both its surroundings and occupants.

Technical constraints on tall buildings are not yet stifling. Structural systems to deal with buildings more than 400 metres (1,300 feet) high are readily evolving. Malaysian regulations allow deeper floor plates than would be common in the West, so the height of these towers can be achieved within a moderate slenderness ratio of 1 to 8.6 – a measure of width to height useful when making comparisons. The standard check

on structural efficiency is a division of the structural weight by the usable floor area. Typically this quotient decreases with increasing building height, rising again beyond the 30-storey mark. Very tall towers embody a lot of material and energy within their fabric compared with four- or five-storey low rise. Statistics on construction speed indicate that 200-metre (655-foot)-high buildings can be completed at a rate of a floor every three days; however, the five-year construction phase of the Petronas Towers equates to a floor every five days. Super-tall buildings are expensive and extend the disruption of construction.

The building armature comprises a megaframe of reinforced concrete and steel. The vertical loadbearing elements, core and 16 perimeter megacolumns, are all in high-strength concrete, and will settle together over the building's life so that – except in the façade – movement provisions are unnecessary. Floors are steel-framed, supporting concrete slabs. The wide, square central shaft of vertical circulation is connected to the perimeter ring with four levels of trussed-steel outriggers, each set two storeys high. Binding the major structural components together minimizes tensile forces from wind loads. These pulls on the frame require expensive joints and foundation provisions if they are to be resisted.

Concrete in the vertical elements raises the total weight of the building, but the difficult ground conditions of Kuala Lumpur – alluvia over potholed limestone –

Above: Extruded and anodized aluminium pilaster closers, sills and brise-soleil model the building's surface. Specular reflections scatter sunlight and animate the façades.

Above: Feature lighting
picks out the tiers and
facets of the symmetrical
forms. Huge lamps at
ground level reinforce
the well of light reflecting
between the twin towers.

Above: Decoration
and illumination levels
condense as the build-
ings rise culminating in
beacons at the base of
each finial. The mid-level
bridge is underscored
with projected light.

need deep piling and the foundations were not sensitive to overall load. The myriad microcracks in the structural concrete fret when the material is stressed, contributing a high level of energy absorption to the structure. In combination with mass at high level, reducing the response of the building to buffeting, this intrinsic damping is sufficient to keep the dynamic behaviour of the building within acceptable limits – mechanical dampers are unnecessary.

This megastructure plays no part in the building's expression. Twin towers provide the requisite floor space, given the allowable floor widths. Their profiles are ideally suited to a vertical transportation system that delivers 12,000 workers daily. Double-decker lifts increase capacities and the sky-lobby system of express lifts to local distributors is expanded by the provision of the high-level link bridge. A strong visual feature on the project building, this clever piece of engineering deals gracefully with the large relative movements high up on the two swaying towers. Two articulated walkways span out to meet on a central ring, supported independently back down onto either side by slender struts.

The indigenous signature of the building is generated by the plan. Originally a 12-pointed star in the competition entry, the layout was nuanced by alternating angular and rounded cantilever bays to make an 'ad quadratum' device of eight corners. This motif, widespread in the Muslim world, also found its way round medieval Europe, carried on the twelfth-century flow of knowledge from the Arabic world.

Masons would use it as a geometric tool, to proportion spires and pinnacles. Applied to the profile of the Petronas Towers, it yields the tiered silhouette common to the South-east Asian stupa and tiara temples of the several major religions of the area. Serried ranks of wide aluminium cornices add to the effect. Windows are shaded from the heat by the overhangs, and a reassuring shelf is provided beyond the glass line. The horizontal edges are underlit at night, to register the pagoda effect. The panellized façade system has joints to allow the main frame to bend in the wind and settle in the long term. The cornices shield the horizontal junctions and mullion lines are suppressed, so that their zigzagging rims flute the tower shafts, emphasizing the complex plan shape.

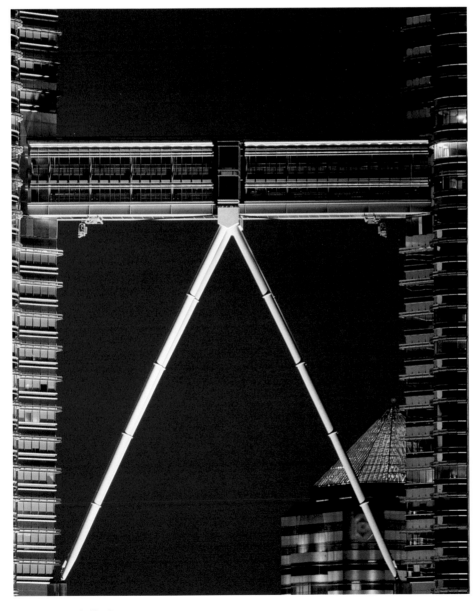

Above: The link bridge is supported on a central collar and articulated at each bearing. Sliding joints allow the towers to sway independently without transferring forces.

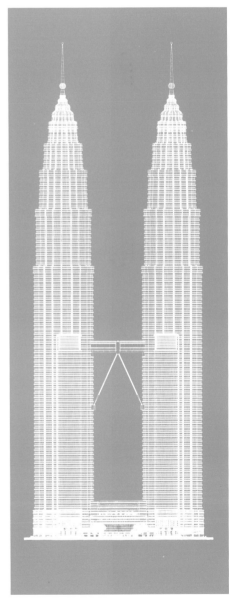

Above: The podium and linked sky lobbies unite the two towers into a single complex. The space between is proportioned to hold the composition together.

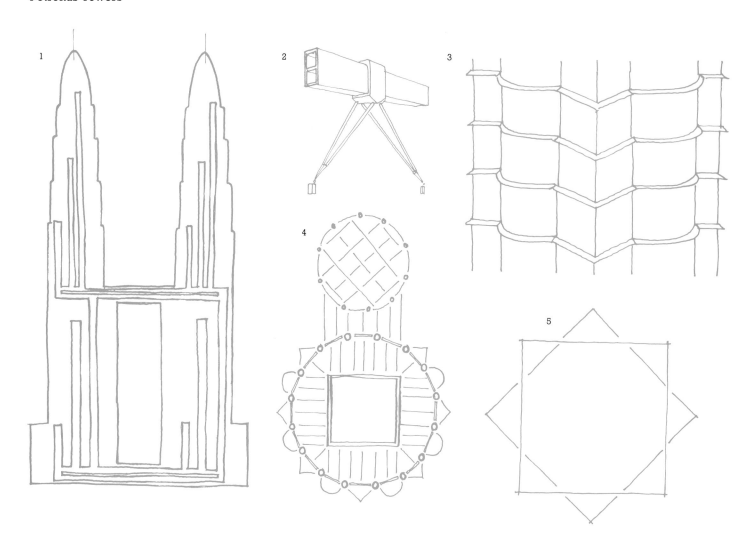

1. Vertical circulation – express lifts and local distributors – are interconnected into a network, uniting the two halves of the form.

2. The central bridge-link comprises two double-decker spans supported on a central collar. The assembly can expand, contract and rotate.

3. The strong horizontals of the sills and brise-soleil contour the elevations. The alternating pattern of curves and corners is achieved with standard jointing.

4. The main frame comprises a ring of super-columns surrounding a square core. The perimeter complexity is dealt with by secondary framing.

5. The 'ad-quadratum' figure from which the plan is generated. Adopted as an Islamic motif, the use of this geometric figure was once widespread in both East and West.

Above: The main entrance and public lobbies are detailed and lit to match the design of the exterior. Mirror-finish mouldings and glass panels line the common areas.

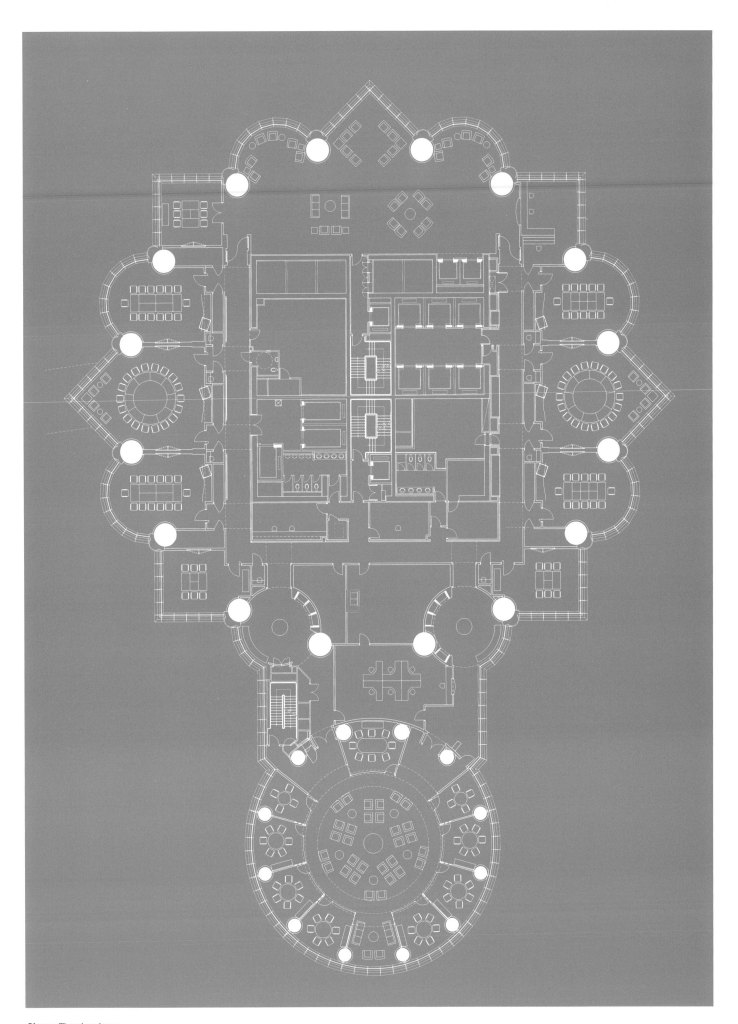

Above: The plan shape, expensive in structure and envelope, produces a variety of well-proportioned spaces and room arrangements. Local circulation is efficient and legible.

BUILDING	MENARA UMNO
LOCATION	PENANG ISLAND, MALAYSIA, 1998
ARCHITECT	T. R. HAMZAH AND YEANG
ENGINEER	TAHIR WONG

Tall building in South-east Asia has so far failed to produce an urbanism equivalent to that of the North American cities. Instead, towers have grown vast, planted in sprawling building complexes, bounded and isolated within their surrounding cities. In reaction, initiatives addressing wider environmental concerns have tended to be coupled with a search for a 'real' indigenous architecture, an expression of the local environment.

Through writing and built example the Malaysian architect and academic Ken Yeang has sought to develop a coherent theory for high rise: the 'bioclimatic' skyscraper. Applying a consistent set of ecological principles to tall-building design will produce forms reflecting their environment. Morphology combines with a sustainability agenda, the careful management and husbanding of resources on behalf of future generations.

Menara UMNO, a 21-floor office block set in a low-density area of the city of Penang, is a relatively small building, the latest in a series of medium-sized towers incorporating Yeang's ideas. The building is conceived as a microcosm of the city, so that the architectural whole evaporates and the project can be deliberately treated as an

agglomeration of disparate elements. The form of the structure is broken up by extensive balcony areas and external routes, with stairs providing local links between floors. Circulation patterns and energy transfers across the building are visualized as if they belonged to an urban block.

The intention is to create new patterns of usage. Such buildings are to be inhabited, moved around in, and therefore inclusive of all the amenities needed across a day or even weeks. Although highly differentiated, the overall organization is intended to have a homogeneity aimed at precluding social segregation and alienation. Health is to be maintained by a close contact with nature through 'sky gardens'– heavily planted external spaces capable of creating a micro-climate immediately adjacent to the building. Dispersed at regular intervals they form nodes within the open 'weave' of the building mass. The idea extrapolates into that of 'green façades'– hanging gardens that act as windbreaks and shading to the face of the building, natural buffers to the environment and potential refuges for birds returning to the city. Planting in a building thus becomes a complete system of 'vertical landscaping'.

Above: The collaged profile of the tower and its segmentation give it a scale appropriate to the variety of building type that makes up old and new Penang city.

176

Above: Lifts and stairwells are amalgamated into a solid sunshield that buffers the accommodation behind from excessive heat and glare.

177

The podium also segregates further into a range of elements, including retail units, car parking and auditoria. Structurally the composition is held together around a simple concrete frame, with massive columns dividing the spaces indifferently. The main lift-cores brace the tower. Transfer structures – beams and slabs deeper than the ordinary floors – are needed to support the set-backs and cantilevers of the variegated silhouette. They find room in the building's sectional organization above the sky gardens and open decks dividing the formal elements. The very ad-hocness of some Asian building construction work enables this sort of building to be successfully detailed.

The easy openness of the structural frame is not particularly efficient, raising the height and therefore cost of the building without adding any usable volume. Adding 200 millimetres (8 inches) onto the depth of a floor to increase the spans of the column grid and edge cantilevers loses a storey height in a 20-storey tower. Here, however, the frame may be seen as a first step towards an undifferentiated armature – not the universal megastructure posited by the architectural thinkers called the Metabolists, but instead a benign use of material imparting relatively little entropy, keeping it available for modification and re-use rather than demolition and destruction.

The project was the first in Malaysia that attempted to condition all its floor space naturally. No seat is more than 6.5 metres (21 feet) from daylight and natural ventilation. Tall 'air walls' – wind-catching elements to amplify cooling breezes – cleave the building's profile. A full air-conditioning system backs up these innovations just in case. Internally the concrete soffits are left unlined, exposing the thermal storage capacity of the main frame. The heavy concrete, gently absorbing and reradiating energy, smoothes out peaks and troughs of temperature.

The profusion of horizontal surfaces makes rain water readily collectable. Run-off

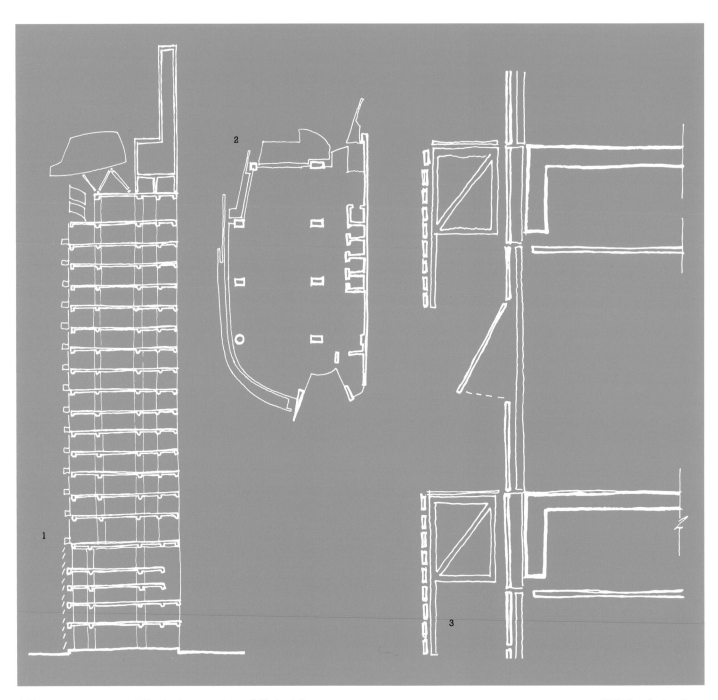

1. The structure comprises an in-situ cast reinforced-concrete frame. Storey heights vary to accommodate the transfer beams required to carry the sections.

2. The simple construction of columns and flat slabs, braced by cross-walls and lift shaft, permit the floors to cantilever outwards to a shaped edge profile.

3. The basic frame supports a series of steel elements, stair gantries, canopies and screens, appended to the main frame. Overhangs and fin-walls shade and shelter terraces and balconies.

Right: In order to reduce lift use, local circulation on foot between floors is encouraged. External stairs linking terraces provide views out to the sea.

and weathering are controlled, and grey water appropriated for flushing and plant irrigation. Although not yet exploited in this scheme, the planes and cornices of the building can act as chassis for photovoltaic cells generating energy from the insolation falling onto the shading systems.

The informality of the building's composition disguises its fully developed aesthetic. Elements are visually balanced with bolt-on details and surface treatments contributing to appearance and humanizing scale. The design harks back to the profuse,

inclusive, urbanism of the old colonies. The verandas and balconies confound the hermetic indifference of the smooth glass shards of globalization rising nearby. This is a developing indigenous architecture. The building may be too small for many of its ideas to work properly, or indeed at all, but its interest lies in its transitional status in the thought of Yeang et al. When the time comes to build at a scale capable of activating these mechanisms, they may still carry something real of the old indigenous forms belonging to their place.

Above: Secondary frames are appended to the main structure, carrying service enclosures and decking to add external spaces.

Above: Sunscreens are
bolted to slab edges and
spandrels to shade the
concrete frame. The zone
between louvres and
external wall acts as a
stack carrying warm air
up and away.

BUILDING   BURJ AL ARAB HOTEL
LOCATION   DUBAI, UNITED ARAB
              EMIRATES, 1996
ARCHITECT   W.S. ATKINS AND PARTNERS
ENGINEER   W.S. ATKINS AND PARTNERS

Above: The design
makes spectacular use
of its structural elements.
The atrium is enclosed
within a Teflon-veneered
glass-fibre-fabric
membrane.

Jay Pritzker realized that the American salesman could live happily ever after. Within six years of Arthur Miller's celebrated play appearing, this second-generation Russian entrepreneur began to establish a series of hotels convenient for airports, with sufficient amenities to combine work and leisure in a short, self-contained break. The Hyatt chain of hotels was born: rep's hostel meets resort hotel. Earlier retirement, and the premium that age sets on luxury, fuelled the rise in hotel standards. The architect John Portman added a new design dimension to the holiday hotel, developing the genre into a hermetic environment almost totally independent of its surroundings. Luxury rooms clustered inwards, onto and above soaring atria.

The Burj Al Arab, the first 'six star' hotel in the world, is a tower built in one of the most hostile environments on earth, without the constraints of an established tradition of building type. A modern pleasure palace, it springs from a man-made island in the Persian Gulf, beside the desert. The place is a completely self-contained entertainment complex, scaled to overwhelm. The artificiality of the 'playground' atmosphere is intentional. The building is as independent of its location as an ocean liner.

The tower is a braced, framed structure comprising two wings of bedroom accommodation, meeting at right angles on the main vertical circulation core and embracing a lofty, east-facing atrium area. The third side of the atrium is closed with a huge screen of architectural membrane. Bowed outwards by steel transom-beams suspended from the apex of the tower, this fabric wall mimics – in a rather strait-laced way – the billowing spinnakers of passing yachts. Its horizontal arches resist wind loads, and the cloth stretched between these meridians is patterned and stressed so as to become a series of rigid double-curved panels: 'hyperbolic paraboloids' – pure forms set in their lowest energy state, and therefore reposing in perfect stability. The Teflon-veneered glass-fibre fabric, always white, transmits about 15 per cent of incident light. In daylight, the atrium is bright and airy, without the glare of the nearby desert. At night, the interior glow reflects across the Gulf. Cantilevered access

Above: On an artificial island in the Persian Gulf, the resort hotel becomes a completely hermetic environment resting on stilts carried through the surrounding breakwater.

balconies open onto this air-conditioned 'oasis' at the heart of the building, making orientation easy and focusing the guests' attention on the merchandise laid out on the main floor.

The cellular nature of a hotel building – all cross-walls, acoustic partitions and vertical risers – is exploited here to produce a framing layout with columns at relatively close centres. Overall weight decreases with the resulting shallower floor beams, reducing total height and allowing plenty of room for service ducts. The dispersed pattern of supports allows the foundations to be manageable: pile sections readily installed by barge into the firm sandbed, independent of the surrounding reclamation works. The island fill could thus be completed without extraordinary provision for long-term settlement.

The detailing of the building has a rather piecemeal character, as if the effort of the specialist subcontractors – employed on the contract to design and install their own packages of work: glass, membrane,

and cladding, all to the latest standards – had not been matched by the care taken to interface between these elements. The utilitarian base structure is decorated with a large external frame, a stylized assemblage of curving elements braced with openwork diagonals like wind-surfing booms. This superflous device tapers into a finial extending upwards. A panoramic restaurant facing out to sea is treated as an independent form, notched in at high level on a huge cantilever. A helipad, an awkward landing threshold in the desert updraughts, is bracketed out above the atrium.

The design was subjected extensively to wind-tunnel testing. Sited just offshore, advantage could be taken of the cooling effect of littoral breezes. These winds rebalance energy between land and sea, and the desert heat can make them so fierce that preventing the infiltration of dust and sand becomes a difficult problem. Tests identify pressures around the complicated shapes of the building layout, which are then used to check the overall stability of the tower and

the adequacy of the finer elements – particularly the fabric membrane.

The likely impact of the interior environment is also an important parameter. In this case, air movements in the dominant space within the building needed review. In all atria buildings, fire is a principal concern: very large internal spaces, particularly tall ones, potentially allow for the unimpeded movement of smoke and flames. Modern fire-engineering looks to computer models, which are capable of simulating a blaze of the magnitude permitted by the fire load (i.e. showing what can burn) and then generating the consequences (i.e. showing how it burns). In order to avoid unsightly barriers and screens, a strategy of introducing smoke 'reservoirs' is followed. Voids are provided in the design, which will contain smoke and prevent it from cooling and drifting into surrounding spaces. Automatic vents at high level are used to allow smoke to escape or to draw the fire upwards, controlling it into one area where it can be contained and extinguished.

1. A piled foundation is carried down through the seabed with groups concentrated around the main support points. The reclamation settles around this formation.

2. The form turns away from onshore breezes towards the sun. The helipad is elevated out of the wake of the wind blowing around the building.

3. The braced exoskeleton is set outside the main structure as decoration. The penthouse restaurant cantilevers forward and sideways from its inter-section with the vertical circulation-core.

4.The membrane screen is divided into a series of panels suspended from the apex of the tower. Arched ribs span across the front wall stiffening the cloth like sail battens.

Right: A glass envelope reflects the desert glare. The atrium screen filters about three-quarters of the incident light, giving a bright, evenly lit interior free from overheating.

PROJECT CREDITS
In order of appearance in the book

Wing Tower, Glasgow
Architect: Richard Horden
Client: Glasgow Science Centre
Structural engineer: Buro Happold

Swiss Re Headquarters, London
Architect: Foster and Partners
Client: Swiss Re
Consultants: Gardiner and Theobald, Hilson
Moran Partnership Ltd, BDSP, Ove Arup &
Partners, RWG Associates, Sandy Brown
Associates

London Bridge Tower, London
Architect: Renzo Piano Building Workshop
architects in collaboration with Broadway Malyan
Architects & Designers, London
Client: Sellar Property Group
Consultants: Ove Arup & Partners/Lerch Bates
Associates

Grand Union Building, London
Architect: Richard Rogers Partnership
Client: PDCL (Paddington Development
Corporation Ltd) / Chelsfield plc
Project manager: Mace
Structural engineer: Pell Frischmann
Services engineer: Cundell Johnston & Partners
Cost consultant: Davis Langdon & Everest

Heron Tower, London
Architect: Kohn Pedersen Fox
Client: Heron Group
Property consultants: Insignia Richard Ellis
Structural engineer: Ove Arup & Partners
Services engineer: Foremans
Cost consultant: Davis Langdon & Everest

The Spire of Dublin, Dublin
Architect: Ian Ritchie Architects: Ian Ritchie,
Robin Cross (project architect) Gordon Talbot,
Phil Coffey
Client: Dublin City Council
Structural and services engineers: Arup
Quantity surveyor: Davis Langdon & Everest
Lighting: Ian Ritchie Architects/La Conch
Main contractor: SIAC/Radley Engineering
joint venture
Suppliers: Steel forming - Barnshaw Steel Bending

Tour sans Fin, Paris
Architect: Atelier Jean Nouvel
Client: SCI Tours sans Fin
Structures and foundations: Ove Arup & Partners
Fluids: OTH, Trouvin Ingenierie
Security: Casso Gaudin
Models: Etienne Follenfant, Gerard Vois

Torre Agbar, Barcelona
Architect: Atelier Jean Nouvel
Client: Layetana
Façades: Arnauld De Bussiere
Fluids: Ibering
Acoustics: Estudi Acustic, Higini Arau
Scenography: Ducks, Michel Cova
Lighting design: Yann Kersale
Colour study: Alain Bony
Structural engineers: Brufau/Obiol S.A.

**Hotel Habitat, Hotel Hesperia and Office
Towers, Barcelona**
Architect: Dominique Perrault, Paris
Client: Grup Riusec
Associate architect: Activitats Arquitectoniques
Structural engineer: Brufau I Associats/Pamias
Industrial Engineering

Commerzbank, Frankfurt
Architect: Foster and Partners
Client: Commerzbank
Structural engineer: Ove Arup and Partners
Environmental consultant: RP & K Sozietat
Main contractor: Hochteif AG

Debis House, Potsdamer Platz, Berlin
Architect: Renzo Piano Building Workshop
in association with Christoph Kohlbecker
Client: Daimler-Chrysler AG
Structural engineer: Boll and Partner

Deutsche Post, Bonn
Architect: Murphy/Jahn, Inc.
Client: Deutsche Post Bauen GmbH
Structure/Enclosure: Werner Sobek
Ingenieure GmbH
Energy/Comfort: Transsolar
Energietechnik GmbH
Mechanical systems: Brandi Consult GmbH
Landscape architect: Peter Walker & Partners
Site architect: Heinle, Wischer und Partner
Lighting consultant: L-Plan, Michael Rohde
Lighting art: AIK Expeditions Lumière,
Yann Kersalé
Façade consultant: DS-Plan
Building physics: Horstmann + Berger
Associate landscape architects: Gottfried
Hansjakob, Wolfgang Roth

Colorium, Düsseldorf
Architect: Alsop Architects Ltd, London
Client: Ibing Immobilien Handel GmbH & Co.
Hochhaus KG, Düsseldorf
Structural engineer: Arup GmbH, Düsseldorf
Ground surveyor: Geotechnisches Büro Dr. E.-H.
Müller, Krefeld

Mechanical and electrical engineer: intecplan
GmbH, Düsseldorf
Façade consultant: DS-Plan, Stuttgart
Building physics consultants: Institut für
Bauphysik/DS-Plan, Mülheim
Lighting consultants: Schlotfeldt Licht, Hamburg,
Landscape design: Alsop Architects Ltd, London,
Main structural contractor: Arbeitsgemeinschaft
Hamelmann Heine, Düsseldorf,
Façade manufacturer: Bug-AluTechnic
AG, Austria

Uptown München, Munich
Architects: Ingenhoven Overdiek Architekten,
Düsseldorf
Client: Hines
Structural engineer: Burggraf, Weichinger and
Partner, München
Engineering consultant: Frankfurt (high-rise);
HL-Technik, Munich (campus buildings)
Façade: DS-Plan GmbH, Stuttgart
Light engineering: v. Kardorff Ingenieure, Berlin
Landscape architecture: Prof. Lange, Hamburg
Construction planning: ATP Achammer Tritthardt
+ Partner, München

Bergisel Ski Jump, Innsbruck
Architect: Zaha Hadid Architects, London UK
Client: Austrian Ski Federation
Local firm: Baumeister Ing. Georg Malojer,
Innsbruck, Austria
Project architect: Jan Huebener
Structure: Jane Wernick, London/Christian
Aste, Innsbruck
Services: Technishes Buro Ing.
Heinz Purcher, Schlaming Technishes Buro
Matthias Schrempf, Schlaming
Peter Fiby, Innsbruck
Lighting: Office for Visual Interaction, New York
Ski jump technology: Bauplanungsburo franz
Fuschlslueger, Austria

Twin Towers, Vienna
Architect: Massimiliano Fuksas
Client: Immofinanz Immobilien Anlagen AG,
Vienna and Wienerberger Baustoffindustrie
AG, Vienna
Structural engineer: Büro Thumberger
+ Kressmeier
Facilities project: Altherm, Baden
Façades: Götz GmbH & Co. KG, Würzburg
Cladding: MCP Austria, Vienna
Lighting project: Die Lichtplaner, Innsbruck
Lighting: Philips, Vienna

Montevideo, Rotterdam
Architect: Mecanoo Architecten
Client: ING Real Estate
Structural engineer: ABT

Turning Torso, Malmö
Architect: Santiago Calatrava
Client: HSB, Malmö, Sweden
Structural engineer: Santiago Calatrava SA
Main contractor: NCC, Malmö, Sweden

Stratosphere Tower, Las Vegas
Architect: Gary Wilson
Client: Stratosphere Hotel Casino
Structural engineer: Brent Wright

Condé Nast Tower, New York
Architect: Fox and Fowle Architects
Client: The Durst Organization
Project team: Bruce S. Fowle FAIA, Design
Principal/Daniel J. Kaplan AIA, Project Director
Main contractor: Tishman Construction
Corporation
Consultant: Cosentini Associates (MEP &
Lighting Design)
Structural engineer: Ysrael Seinuk

New York Times Building, New York
Architect: Renzo Piano Building Workshop in
collaboration with Fox and Fowle Architects,
P.C. (New York)
Client: The New York Times / Forest City
Ratner Company
Structural engineer: Thornton-Tomasetti Engineers

AOL Time Warner Center, New York
Architect of record: Skidmore, Owings &
Merrill LLP
Client: Columbus Center LLC/Time Warner
Project management: John Moran, Philip
Palmgren, Katherine Springer
Structural engineer: Cantor Seinuk Group
Civil engineer: Philip Habib & Associates
Mechanical engineer: Cosentini Associates
Landscape architects: Ken Smith Landscape
Architect
Lighting design: Cline, Bettridge, Bernstein
Lighting Design, Inc.
Consultants: Vollmer Associates, LLP

Highcliff, Hong Kong
Architect: Dennis Lau and Ng Chun Man
Architects and Engineers (H.K.) Ltd
Client: Central Management
Structural Engineer: Magnusson Klemencic
Associates/Maunsell Group
Construction Company: Hip Hing Construction
Co. Ltd./Davis Langdon & Seah Intl

International Finance Centre II, Hong Kong
Design Consultant: Cesar Pelli & Associates,
New Haven, Connecticut
Cesar Pelli, Design Principal
Client: Central Waterfront Property Project
Management Company Ltd.

Project principal and collaborating
designer: Fred W. Clarke
Architect of record: Rocco Design Limited
Associate architect/exterior wall: Adamson
Associates
Planner: Masterplan Limited
Urban design consultant: Designscape
International Ltd.
Landscape consultant: Urbis Limited
Structural engineer: Ove Arup & Partners,
Hong Kong
MEP engineer: J. Roger Preston, Ltd.
Quantity surveyors: Levett & Bailey
General contractor: E Man-Sanfield JV
Construction Ltd.

Di Wang Commercial Centre, Shenzhen
Architect: K.Y. Cheung Design Associates
Client: Karbony Investment
Structural engineer: Leslie E. Robertson
Associates/Maunsell

Taipei Financial Centre, Taipei
Architect: C. Y. Lee Partners
Client: Kumagai Gumi/Turner Construction Co.
Structural engineer: Evergreen Consulting
Engineering

Petronas Towers, Kuala Lumpur
Architect: Cesar Pelli and Associates
Client: Kuala Lumpur City Centre Holdings
Sendirian Berhad
Architect of record: KLCC Berhad Architectural
Division, Kuala Lumpur, Malaysia
Associate architect: Adamson Associates,
Toronto, Ontario
Landscape design: Balmori Associates
and NR Associates
Structural engineers: Thornton-Tomasetti
Engineers and Ranhill Bersekutu Sdn. Bhd
MEP engineers: Flack + Kurtz and KTA
Tenaga Sdn. Bhd

Menara UMNO, Penang
Architect: T.R. Hamzah and Yeang
Architect/Planner: Kenneth Yeang
Client: South East Asia Development Corp.
Structural engineer: Tahir Wong Sdn Bhd

Burj Al Arab, Dubai
Architect: W.S. Atkins and Partners
Client: Jumeirah Beach Resort
Structural engineer: W.S. Atkins and Partners
Co-contractor: Al Habtoor Engineering
Co-contractor: Fletcher Construction
Co-contractor: Murray & Roberts
Steel construction: Eversendai Engineering
Subcontractor: DOKA (formwork)
Subcontractor: TYCSA
Lifting: VSL International

INDEX

Page numbers in *italics* refer to illustrations

PICTURE CREDITS

Corbis/Historical Picture Archive **7**
Corbis/Dave Bartruff **8**
Corbis/Bettmann **10**
Corbis/Angelo Hornak **12L**
Arcaid/Niall Clutton **12R**
Arcaid/John Edward Linden **13**
Arcaid/Mark Fiennes **15L**
Arcaid/Ezra Stoller **15R**
Arcaid/Ezra Stoller **16**
Arcaid/Peter Aaron **17**
Corbis/Bettmann **18L**
Kevin Roche John Dinkeloo
and Associates LLC **18R**
Arcaid/Bill Tingey **19L**
Arcaid/Alex Bartel **19R**
Future Systems **21**
Arcblue/Keith Hunter **24, 26/27, 28**
View/Grant Smith **31**
View/Peter MacKinven **33**
View/Dennis Gilbert **35**
Renzo Piano Building Workshop/Hays
Davidson & John McLean **36**
Renzo Piano Building Workshop/
Frederic Terreaux **38/39**
Richard Rogers Partnership/
Eamonn O'Mahony **42L**
Richard Rogers Partnership/
Hayes Davidson **42/43**
Richard Rogers Partnership/
Eamonn O'Mahony **45**
Images courtesy of KPF/
Hayes Davidson, GMJ **49, 51, 53**
Ian Ritchie Architects/Barry Mason **54**
Atelier Jean Nouvel/Georges Fessy/©ADAGP,
Paris and DACS, London 2005 **58, 59, 61**
Atelier Jean Nouvel/©ADAGP, Paris and DACS,
London 2005 **62, 63, 64**, Artefactory **67, 68/69**
View/Dennis Gilbert **65**
Dominique Perrault Architecte ©ADAGP,
Paris and DACS, London 2005 **70, 71, 72**
View/Dennis Gilbert **74**
Foster and Partners /Nigel Young **75,77, 78T**
View/Dennis Gilbert **78B**
Foster and Partners/Ian Lambot **79**
Renzo Piano Building Workshop/Cano Enrico **80**
Renzo Piano Building Workshop/
Mosch Vincent **81**
Renzo Piano Building Workshop/
Berengo Gardin Gianni **83, 85**
Murphy Jahn/Andreas Keller **87**
Murphy Jahn/Josef Gartner **88**
Murphy Jahn **89B**
Murphy Jahn /HG Esch **89T**

Murphy Jahn/Deutsche Post Andreas Keller **90,91**
View/Dennis Gilbert **92/3, 94**
Ingenhoven Overdiek Architekten/
H. G. Esch, Hennef **98, 101, 102**
Zaha Hadid Architects/Hélène Binet
105, 106, 107, 109
M. Fuksas/Angelo Kaunat **110**
M. Fuksas/Rupert Steiner **111**
M. Fuksas/A. Furudate **112**
M. Fuksas/Angelo Kaunat **115**
Mecanoo Architecten b.v **116, 117**
Santiago Calatrava SA **121**
Courtesy of NCC AB **123L**
Courtesy of NCC AB **123R**
Santiago Calatrava **125**
Corbis/Joseph Sohm; ChromoSohm Inc **126/127**
Corbis/Richard Cummins **129**
Corbis/Gunter Marx Photography **130**
Arcaid/ Neil Troiano **132/133**
ESTO/Jeff Goldberg **135, 136**
Renzo Piano Workshop/Michel Denance **139**
Renzo Piano Workshop/Michel Denance **141**
SOM **143, 144, 147**
Dennis Lau & Ng Chun Man **148,149,151,152,153**
Cesar Pelli & Associates Architects/Virgile Simon
Bertrand **154, 155**
IFC Development Limited **157, 158, 159,**
American Design **160, 161, 163, 164, 165**
AFP/Getty Images/ Patrick Lin **166/167**
EPA/PA Photos **169**
ESTO/Jeff Goldberg **170, 171, 172, 173, 174**
Courtesy of T.R. Hamzah & Ken Yeang **176, 177,
179, 180, 181**
Chris Caldicott **182, 183, 185**

AUTHOR'S ACKNOWLEDGEMENTS

The following architects and engineers were
kind enough to allow me to interview them
about projects featured in the book: K. Y.
Cheung (Di Wang Centre, Shenzen), Fred
Pilbrow (Heron Tower, London), David Dumigan
and Greg Sang (IFC II, Hong Kong), Richard
Horden (Wing Tower, Glasgow) and Cristina
Garcia (for information on Spanish examples).
I would also like to thank project editor Mark
Fletcher, designer Neil Pereira, picture
researcher Claire Gouldstone, researcher
Della Pearlman at Techniker, and Philip Cooper
and Liz Faber at Laurence King.